IT IS NOT YOUR BUSINESS TO SUCCEED

*Your Role in Leadership When
You Can't Control Your Outcomes*

———✦———

BRANDON M. WEST

Copyright © 2023 by Brandon West. All rights reserved.

Published by ZOE Publishing Studio, Gainesville, FL.

For editing information, visit GoodCommaEditing.com.

ISBN 979-8-9894241-0-8 (hardcover)
ISBN 979-8-9894241-1-5 (paperback)
ISBN 979-8-9894241-2-2 (ebook)

Unless otherwise indicated, Scripture quotations are from The ESV® Bible (The Holy Bible, English Standard Version®), copyright © 2001 by Crossway, a publishing ministry of Good News Publishers. Used by permission. All rights reserved.

Scripture quotations marked (NASB) are taken from the (NASB®) New American Standard Bible®, Copyright © 1960, 1971, 1977, 1995, 2020 by The Lockman Foundation. Used by permission. All rights reserved. Lockman.org.

Designed by Jenelle Kruse at PHOS Creative.

To my mom, Diane Hall, who led the way with writing. Her book, Giggles with Grandma, is a book about Parkinson's Disease meant to be a lighter way to look at Parkinson's through the eyes of a child. You were a warrior, an inspiration, and a support to me in every way.

To my wife, Shelley West, for your constant faithfulness in our marriage, parenting, and during the process of writing this book. To many more writing-retreat vacations as we explore the world together.

To my children, Parker and Landen. I long for nothing more in your lives than that you act justly, love faithfulness, and walk humbly with your God. Redefine what success means, don't neglect your gifts, keep a close watch on yourselves, and be faithful to the end (1 Timothy 4:12–16).

CONTENTS

Reality Redefinition — 7

SUCCESS IS BROKEN
1. The Fatal Flaw of Outcome-Based Thinking — 11

A NEW PARADIGM
2. Redefining Success — 25
3. The One Called Faithful and True — 39
4. The Daily Hard Work of Faithfulness — 53

THE LIFESTYLE OF A FAITHFUL LEADER
5. Surrender — 73
6. Becoming — 93
7. Stewardship — 113
8. Perseverance — 133

AN ETERNAL CALLING
9. God Is Pleased with You — 159
10. How Then Shall We Live? — 175

Notes — 193

Introduction

REALITY REDEFINITION

I am a failure.

I have dreamed dreams I've never accomplished, started things I've never finished, taken risks that have wasted resources, and attempted things that have regularly flatlined. So I've regularly told myself *I am a failure.*

Alongside a killer team, I've had the privilege of building a digital marketing agency that serves clients all across the US. We've won awards for our growth, our culture, and our work, and we've been recognized by our chamber of commerce and *Florida Trend* magazine for being one of the best workplaces in our state.

But, regardless of any "success" I've had, it never ceases to amaze me how the loss of a single client, the resignation of a key team member, a dry sales funnel, a red month, or a missed leadership moment can cause that same sense of failure to come flooding back into my heart.

I've consulted with hundreds of leaders across almost every marketplace sector, and, in every one, I found this to be true: **our definitions of failure and success are broken**.

We are drowning under an infinite deluge of definitions for what success is supposed to mean in our lives. And, when we don't live up to those false standards, our feelings of purpose, identity, and value are wrongly eroded or, at times, completely destroyed. The resulting personal, relational, and professional implications are devastating to leaders.

I wrote this book because I need it. As my wife read this book for the first time, she left a comment on one section that said, "Babe. Mic drop! Can I remind you of this later?" I need to be reminded regularly to adjust my definition of success, to lift my eyes off of my outcomes, and to set them on a higher target.

This book isn't just a shift in mindset; it's a redefinition of reality.

We'll explore the definitions of success we're being sold, why they're wrong, and how they're harming us. We'll examine a whole new definition of success, inspiring examples of people living that out, and what it looks like for us to realign our journey to this new reality.

Like a recovering addict, I frequently relapse into the failure/success mindset. Each time I do, I must make a conscious effort to return to a healthier frame of mind. And, with every recovery, I discover deeper joy and freedom in both my life and leadership.

Friend, it is not your business to succeed. If you will surrender to that truth, you will live, lead, and love from a powerful place, for a powerful purpose. Let's go there together.

SUCCESS IS BROKEN

Most people are more comfortable with old problems than new solutions.[1]

JOHN C. MAXWELL

1

THE FATAL FLAW OF OUTCOME-BASED THINKING

Our greatest fear should not be of failure but of succeeding at things in life that don't really matter.

FRANCIS CHAN

ONE QUESTION HAS haunted me in leadership for *years*. The question was presented to me during our leadership development program at PHOS Creative, the digital marketing agency I founded. In one of our meetings, as we discussed the challenges of leadership, one of our team members asked, "How do you measure the success of a leader?"

How do you tell a successful leader from an unsuccessful leader?

I know of only one way, and we use it all the time.

INTRODUCING THE OUTCOME-BASED MINDSET

When we talk about the important character qualities of a leader, we talk about things like integrity and trustworthiness. But who are the successful leaders our culture exalts in the media and honors in our storytelling? Who are the leaders we lift up, saying, "These people are successful"? Integrity and trustworthiness typically have nothing to do with those people.

Our choice of which leaders we praise as a culture reveals what we really value in leaders.

Google "successful people," and the results will be men and women who . . .

1. Made a fortune [Money]
2. Have a business that has recently been appraised or sold at a staggering figure [Business Value]
3. Won a prestigious award, medal, or trophy [Fame]

These leaders are deemed successful because of their actions or accomplishments. They are successful leaders not because of their character but because of the outcomes of the things they've worked on.

I call this the "outcome-based mindset," and it permeates most of the way we define success.

This outcome-based thinking makes its way into our lives as well. We realize we might not be as "successful" as these public figures, but we tell ourselves we'll be successful when we . . .

1. Reach a certain amount of annual income
2. Save a certain amount for retirement
3. Own a certain thing (house, car, boat, plane, etc.)
4. Have a certain number of followers on Instagram
5. Win a certain award
6. Start a family with a certain number of kids
7. Travel to an exotic country (or live there)

Reaching these outcomes becomes our definition of success. If we make these things happen, we will believe that we have "made it."

This thinking can so quickly begin to persuade every choice we make, attitude we hold, and priority we set. On a day-by-day, meeting-by-meeting, and email-by-email basis, I am tempted to rewrite my definition of success around any one of the above goalposts.

But I have found over and over that this outcome-based mindset creates a world of dangerous and draining problems for each of us.

YOU CANNOT CONTROL YOUR OUTCOMES

For one, the societal systems we live and work in are fragile. Most of the time, we walk around forgetting, disbelieving, or ignoring this reality, but a global pandemic, economic disaster, environmental catastrophe, technological disruption, or political upheaval can quickly remind us that we live in a fragile world.

In the middle of 2020, I learned a term that helped me understand this fragility.

The term *VUCA* was first used by military professionals to characterize the conditions faced by soldiers when they step onto the battlefield. *VUCA* stands for *volatility*, *uncertainty*, *complexity*, and *ambiguity*. That sounds like a war to me. Land mines, drone strikes, snipers, camouflage, and undercover agents produce a volatile, uncertain, complex, and ambiguous operating environment.

Whether we're on the battlefield or in the boardroom, an emergency, catastrophe, or unexpected hardship can remind us that the world we inhabit is characterized by volatility, uncertainty, complexity, and ambiguity.

What a VUCA world teaches is that you cannot control your outcomes. The world we live in is too puzzling and indefinite to be counted upon. Nothing you do can guarantee you will ever achieve the outcomes you are driving for. In a VUCA environment, nothing is certain.

As you pursue your desired income level, what if the markets change and your current skill set is no longer valuable?

As you pursue your retirement or lifestyle goals, what if an unforeseen illness and ensuing medical bills empty your savings accounts?

As you pursue your family goals, what if you are told by your doctor that you will forever be infertile?

As you pursue your travel goals, what if a global pandemic shuts down travel (a crazy thought prior to 2020 that is so real now)?

You cannot guarantee that our VUCA world will not disrupt and destroy the outcomes you have so firmly attached your heart to. If your definition of success is tied to a volatile, uncertain, complex, and ambiguous future, you have hitched yourself to a wagon you can't drive. When our definition of success is tied to our outcomes, which we cannot control, we are destined to fail.

It's a foolish investment with a bad return on investment.

YOU BEGIN TO VALUE THE WRONG THINGS

My wife, Shelley, and I love *Hamilton*, by Lin-Manuel Miranda. We've practically worn out the Broadway movie, listened to the soundtrack countless times, and experienced a live stage performance. Our kids can sing all the king's songs from memory. I even rewrote the opening song to tell the story of "The PHOS Creative Agency" and sang it at our seven-year anniversary celebration.

The internet devised a word to describe fans like us: *Hamilites*.

When Shelley and I watched the movie production the first time, we started it way too late at night. We didn't know what we had just committed ourselves to. (It's 2 hours and 40 minutes long.) When the movie finally finished, we were wide-eyed at 12:30 a.m., unable to go to bed. We were overwhelmed by the powerful lyrical content, stage performance, vocals, lighting, audio mixing, and choreography.

The performance is divided into halves: the first is a powerful story of Alexander Hamilton's non-stop, go-getter, always-fighting lifestyle. The second half is a darker, honest look at the latter parts of his life involving the death of his son, marital infidelity, blackmail, and his vain attempts to protect his reputation.

If you are unfamiliar with the story of Alexander Hamilton, he is pictured on the ten-dollar bill and was one of the Founding Fathers of the United States. Somehow he was both a gifted military leader and an exceptionally gifted writer. (I don't see the connection, but it worked.) He is probably best known for writing 51 of 85 installments of *The Federalist Papers*, which helped to persuade Americans to ratify the Constitution of the United States.

Spending an inordinate amount of time writing, Hamilton eventually put himself into a compromising position that led to a spiral of bad choices, a broken marriage, a loss of influence, and a stained reputation.

Near the end of the first act of the Broadway production, before Hamilton loses himself in his work and has an affair with another man's wife, Hamilton's own wife, Eliza, sings a song over him. She pleads with her husband, trying to convince him that legacy and money aren't important. She essentially begs him, *Write me into your life and let me be a part of your story. Stay here with me instead of leaving our family again. Let that be enough for you.*

I can't help but wonder what Alexander Hamilton's life would have been like if he had listened and yielded to his wife's heart at that moment. What if she had been enough for him, and he had decided to stay with her instead of going to work more? Could his marriage have avoided such pain and heartache?

The first, most obvious follow-up question to this thought, however, is always the same: "Yes, but what would America be like today without everything Alexander accomplished?"

Aye, there's the rub.

Was what Alexander Hamilton accomplished worth what he compromised and sacrificed?

Every decision we make, every endeavor we commit to, every dream we write down, and every strategic plan we create forces us to make decisions about where we will invest our time, talent, and treasure. And we make those choices based on the things we value.

What do you value? What drives the decisions you make for your marriage, your children, and yourself? What are the business values that drive the decisions you make as an organizational leader?

The outcome-based mindset says, "I will do whatever it takes to get what I want, because the last thing I want to do is be a failure, and the last thing I want to experience is the feeling that I have failed." This mindset puts the avoidance of failure above all other values, such as marriage, family, peace, character, etc.

When we tie our identity to our results, we begin to value the wrong things. These new values then require us to make sacrifices to means that are not worth the ends.

You could long to be successful in every way that you think matters only to find out you've been a failure in every area that actually matters.

YOU CREATE MORE PROBLEMS FOR YOURSELF, NOT LESS

Shelley and I were on a date one evening at Whole Foods. FYI, that's what parents of young children do when they are on a date: they go shopping, frequently for groceries.

To get a sense of how successful this date was, let's just say we never actually made it into the store that evening (and not because we were making out in the car).

We were in the middle of one of the most challenging seasons of our marital journey. What made it worse was that the thing coming between us was the very thing we had promised one another would never threaten our marriage. We vowed early on, "No matter how much we have or do not have, we'll never let our finances come between us in our marriage." Unfortunately, the more we made and the more we had, the more we disagreed about how it should be spent. Regular arguments were creeping into our nightly routines, driving a relational wedge between us, and keeping us from greater intimacy and marital joy.

That evening, I had a great plan for our date night and how we would invest in the health of our marriage: we were going to take a life health assessment and discuss the answers together! (The women reading this already know this isn't going to go well.) Lesson learned: I like marriage surveys and assessments to help solve problems; Shelley does not.

The date night discussion questions started off strong:

> Question 1: How's your walk with God? *Doing pretty well so far. Good dialogue.*
>
> Question 2: How's your parenting going? *This one hurt a little.*
>
> Question 3: How's your marriage health? *Houston, we have a problem.*
>
> Question 4: How's your personal financial management going? . . .

That's as far as we got in this eight-question survey as disagreements and arguments ensued.

The one thing we said would never divide us was now creating disunity, resentment, and distance in our relationship. It was causing hurt feelings, a sense of loneliness, the cold shoulder, and tears.

Being "successful" didn't solve our problems. It created new ones.

I think this is a common mindset: *When I achieve success, I won't let it affect my marriage. My heart is stronger than that. My spouse and I are more united and on-mission together about finances and how we want to use them than the people I've heard these stories about.*

You've been told regularly, "Money, wealth, fame, and power won't solve your problems," but you think, *I'm different. I can be different.*

We read things like "the rich man [will] fade away in the midst of his pursuits" (James 1:11), and we think, *That won't be me.*

Let me just tell you: you are not as strong as you think.

This is more of a challenge than you realize.

It's more of a challenge because drift happens more slowly than you expect it will. It is the small things that slowly, over time, month over month, year over year erode the commitments we have to simple, steadfast living.

To have a lot of money or stuff and believe that you'll never fall prey to the dangers that accumulation and success bring in your life is like believing you can regularly engage in heavy alcohol use and not become an alcoholic.

Success defined by money and possessions will not deliver on its promises, because enough is never enough.

YOU GET DISTRACTED FROM THINGS THAT REALLY MATTER

In the early years of building PHOS, I was living the all-in entrepreneurial life.

As I was building my team, I had one simple goal: I wanted people to tell me unprompted that this was the best job they'd ever had. The counsel I was receiving about leadership had me fully bought in to the idea that "culture eats strategy for breakfast," and I wanted to do everything I could to make my people happy.

We started hosting weekly lunch dates, annual Christmas gatherings, birthday parties, creative team-building activities, and wildly extra anniversary celebrations for the team. The office was intentionally decorated, thank-you gifts for team members were strategically purchased, and team meetings were deliberately designed to help us fuel our hoped-for future. I poured myself into every meticulous detail.

One night after I came home from work, Shelley and I were debriefing our days in the kitchen. As I told her about some cool thing I had done again for someone at work to make them feel special, I could feel Shelley getting increasingly cold in her body language.

With some pain in her voice, she asked me, "What if you worked as hard to be creative at home as you did at work?"

Heart. Broken.

Shelley saw all the cool things I was doing with my time and was questioning, "Are you going to do that for us?" The people that mattered to me most were left wanting for affection while I chased the wrong outcomes.

I've seen it in my life and the lives of countless leaders: **the outcome-based mindset rewires our priorities, pleads with us to do whatever is needed to achieve what we want, and distracts us from the things that really matter.**

When your sense of identity and worth hinge on your achievements and output, you will find yourself doing anything to keep that boat from sinking—sacrificing whatever it takes to avoid being labeled a failure, all in the relentless pursuit of "results, results, results."

The results we're chasing are simply not worth the harm we cause to the people who matter most.

A DIFFERENT WAY OF THINKING

If success is one of the three things listed above (money, business valuation, or fame), and you don't have one of those listed on your LinkedIn profile, are you a failure?

If you're an honest, normal business owner or leader, you ask yourself this regularly. You wonder things like *Why is my business, organization, team, or ministry not growing like I thought it would? Am I the problem in this? Am I the ceiling that is preventing this from going as far as it could go? Am I a failure?*

If we buy into the idea that success is defined by money, business valuation, and/or fame, we'll subject ourselves to a never-ending torrent of soul-destroying expectations to attain these results. In the end, we'll find ourselves grappling with far weightier issues than just our failure to reach our ill-defined definition of "success":

Exhaustion	Emotional Depletion
Burnout	Callousness
Depression/Anxiety	Dissatisfaction
Lack of Purpose	Lack of Boundaries
Feelings of Inadequacy	Overwhelming Weight of Responsibility
Disappointment	
Restlessness	Fear
Frustration	Identity Crises

Maybe you're trying hard to create success right now. Maybe you're working on building multiple streams of income. Maybe you've started multiple businesses in an attempt to figure out which one will work.

You're trying so hard to make it happen because you've got to do anything it takes to attach that label to yourself: "I am a successful person." But you're burnt out and discouraged. You've been grinding, and now you feel ground up. You're overwhelmed because you've tried it all and you don't know what to do next.

Or maybe you've already accomplished a lot (you have the wealth, business value, and fame), but you're thinking, *Shouldn't there be more to owning a business or leading an organization? Is my future really just about more money, more equity, and more awards?*

Our current model for success is broken.

We are experiencing all the struggles listed above because we have tied our definition of success to things we can't control, things that demand we give up what truly matters, and things that create more challenges than solutions.

This is the outcome-based mindset, and it has doomed us to failure.

There are two types of success: one that matters and one that does not. To move forward, you will need to redefine your understanding of success.

Once we discover this renewed perspective, we'll experience greater freedom, a profound sense of purpose, and an elevated calling. Although this alternative mindset may be less common than the conventional outcome-based mindset for success, its rewards are far more fulfilling.

So, what is success?

A NEW PARADIGM

He has told you, O man, what is good;
and what does the LORD require of you
but to do justice, and to love kindness,
and to walk humbly with your God?

MICAH 6:8

2

REDEFINING SUCCESS

It is not your business to succeed (no one can be sure of that) but to do right: when you have done so, the rest lies with God.

C. S. LEWIS

I **HAD A VERY DIFFERENT** view of parenting before I was actually a parent. Years before I had kids, I was shopping at a local grocery store where I witnessed a mother pushing her two kids in one of those fun, green, car-looking shopping carts. As she was about to enter an aisle, I watched as her kids screamed at her, red in the face, hands clenched, about ready to pop a blood vessel in their foreheads.

Ignorantly, I thought to myself, *Just take them outside, discipline them in the car, then come back in, and everything will be fine.*

Then I had kids.

Over the past 15 years, I have found that no matter how well I parent my children, I cannot ultimately control them or their outcomes.

We have diligently loved and led our kids. We have encouraged them and corrected them. We have taught them, reminded them, then reminded them again and again and again and again. We have invested (and will continue to invest) ourselves into our children. But I cannot ensure that, just because I did so, my desired future for them will happen.

Answer this question: what is a successful parent?

If *Success* magazine had a cover story about the world's most "successful parents," what story would it share? Would it not contain a powerful story about how these parents' children never struggled with drugs, went to jail, or totaled their cars, and they now all have their own beautiful families, large incomes, yachts, and loads of influence?

Is parental success contingent on each of your children turning out to be everything you've ever dreamed?

If so, the majority of us are doomed to be failures as parents. You can't control your children's futures. You can't just take them out to the car, have a stern conversation with them, bring them back into grandma's house, and expect them never to disobey again.

But if we can't measure successful parenting by outcomes, how can we measure it? And if you can't control the outcomes of children, what does it mean to be a successful parent?

If you can't control the outcomes of your ministry, what does it mean to be a successful pastor?

If you can't control the outcomes of your business, what does it mean to be a successful leader?

SIMULTANEOUSLY FRUSTRATED AND FREE

This is difficult to hear, but **you can do everything right and still fail to achieve the outcomes you desire.** Outcomes are in the Lord's hands—not ours.

> The horse is made ready for the day of battle, but the victory belongs to the LORD. (Proverbs 21:31)

> Unless the LORD builds the house, those who build it labor in vain. Unless the LORD watches over the city, the watchman stays awake in vain. (Psalm 127:1)
>
> Many are the plans in the mind of a man, but it is the purpose of the LORD that will stand. (Proverbs 19:21)

The plans could be made, the watchmen could be up all night on guard, the horses could be prepared with your best war gear, and you could still lose the war.

Your victory belongs to the Lord.

Your *outcomes* belong to the Lord.

I find myself having two competing reactions to these truths.

On the one hand, I'm frustrated. I'm frustrated because I've seen this story play out so many times in my life.

On July 25, 2023, I was finishing brushing my teeth when the Gainesville Police Department knocked on my front door. Two officers informed me that my business had been broken into the night before. I thanked them for coming, but I told them this was probably a mistake, as we had experienced several false alarms in the prior months.

I pulled out my phone, and there were no alarm notifications. *Good sign.* But, as I began to scrub through the video footage from the previous night with the officers, we watched several clips of a masked man walking in and out of PHOS for 16 minutes with handfuls of our laptops, desktops, cameras, lenses, and drives.

I couldn't drive to the studio fast enough as I anxiously wondered how much had actually been stolen.

When I arrived, I walked up to thousands of glass pieces covering the ground. Underneath my shoes, I could hear the crunching as I squeezed through the broken area in the door onto more shards that covered our cafeteria floors, tables, and benches. I walked through the studio with the officers and detectives reviewing the crime scene and trying to determine the totality of the theft.

In the end, we identified $30,000 worth of missing gear. Our insurance rep showed up to inform us that our policy didn't include coverage for theft. The security company told us they had no liability because the entry sensor wasn't triggered, our motion sensor was hung too high, and our glass-break sensor had run out of battery.

Everything was failing, and I was frustrated.

The word I kept thinking of over and over was *wasted*. This felt like such a poor use of our time, energy, and resources. We have a vision for using this business and our profits for the Kingdom, and I felt like my reward for doing so was robbery. Every item that we realized was missing only fed into my feelings about this apparent waste.

When one of the pastors at my church heard what was going on, he dropped everything he had on his schedule and texted me, "I'm on my way." After we walked through the space together, he turned to me in the conference room, placed his hand firmly on my shoulder, and said with an unshakable confidence in his voice: "God is going to use this situation."

Over the next week, my frustration slowly turned to freedom as I began to see that reminder play out. I started a note in my phone that I populated for the next two weeks with every instance I saw God show up in the middle of this situation. I felt free because I knew God was at work, and that He was leveraging this seemingly wasted moment for His purposes.

This wasn't an outcome for PHOS that I would have chosen. This wasn't even an outcome that I would define as good, but God still meant it for good.

While it's frustrating to know that our outcomes in life are ultimately out of our control, it's equally *freeing*.

If you are not the ultimate arbiter of outcomes, then you have a different role to play in the disasters you navigate, the decisions you make, the new ventures you pursue, and the risks you take.

As a recovering control freak, knowing that my outcomes are outside of my control is both frustrating and freeing, *but would I really want to have it any other way?*

A TALE OF TWO MINDSETS

If our role in life is not to work at all costs to control our outcomes, then what is the role we play? I love this thought by C. S. Lewis:

> There is always some peace in having submitted to the right. Don't spoil it by worrying about the *results*, if you can help it. It is not your business to succeed (no one can be sure of that) but to do right: when you have done so, the rest lies with God.[2]

What's your role in life with your outcomes? Do right, then leave the results with God.

That's it? Yep.

This way of thinking is a new mindset. It is the **faithfulness mindset**.

Oh, how the outcome-based mindset despises this way of thinking! Let's compare these two mindsets:

	Outcome-Based Mindset	Faithfulness Mindset
Achievement	I am what I achieve.	I work hard and entrust the results to God.
Ability	If I work hard enough, I can accomplish anything I set my mind to.	Apart from God, I can do nothing; He is my strength and gives and takes as He pleases.
Results	I expect positive results from all the hard work I put in; when an initiative goes well, I'm fulfilled, and, when it doesn't, I see myself as a failure.	I trust God to do as He pleases with my work; when it goes well, I thank Him for things I don't deserve, and, when it doesn't, I surrender to His better plan.
Work Ethic	I work as hard as possible because my identity depends on it.	I work hard because the glory of God deserves it.
People	I lead as needed because people are a means to an end.	I lead well because I see leveraging the influence I have with other people as a calling God has on my life.
Waiting	If I'm not getting the results I want in the timeframe I want, I go make things happen for myself.	I'm patient and I wait on God's timing, knowing that He uses seasons of waiting to refine and shape me.
Rest and Retreat	Rest and retreat are unnecessary distractions in my pursuit of achievement.	I see rest and retreat as critical parts of transformation, learning, and recharging.
Marriage and Parenting	I make sacrifices in my marriage and family as necessary to get the outcomes I want in my career and hobbies.	I make the sacrifices necessary in my business and personal interests to ensure my marriage and children maintain priority in my schedule.
Wealth	I work to accumulate as much as I can; I deserve the things I want because of how hard I've worked.	I guard my heart against the lies that wealth speaks to me about my identity, worth, and security, and I practice generous giving.

Fame and Reputation	I enjoy the spotlight as the natural outcome of my success.	If something I do is publicized, I see it as a platform for more ministry, impact, and influence because I am more concerned with God's renown than my own.
Success	If I have great results and outcomes, I am successful.	I am successful if I am faithful, regardless of my outcomes.

As you read through that list, how did you feel? Any lessons learned?

Success isn't about your ratio of good outcomes to bad outcomes. You are not what you produce. Success is about whether or not you have been faithful.

WHAT IS FAITHFULNESS?

Some people could look at such a mindset and say, "This is the mindset of lazy people." They think if we give up a sense of responsibility for our results, we'll sit back, do nothing, and blame our poor results on God, saying, "I guess He didn't want any good results from me today."

They would be right: doing nothing is laziness, not faithfulness.

Faithfulness is daily hard work entrusted to God.

Faithful leaders get up every morning and run toward their calling, trusting that God is in heaven, doing as He pleases (Psalm 115:3). They are eager to see how the Lord will choose to use their faithfulness, knowing that their work has an impact on the lives of those around them.

Yes, the victory of the battle is God's, but you have to get the horses ready.

Yes, the Lord is watching over the city, but you have to stay awake on your shift, keep your eyes open, and warn the city when a threat comes.

In Psalm 144:1, David says that it is God "who trains [his] hands for war, and [his] fingers for battle." David is doing all the training for war, but he acknowledges that it is ultimately God who is preparing and strengthening him.

Faithful leaders are the hardest workers; they just think differently about their work. They go after the hardest work, but they say with every task, "God, you're responsible for the outcomes, and I trust you."

It is not our business to succeed. Our job is to do what is right, then trust God for the results.

The difficulty with such a mindset is the level of surrender that is required to maintain a lifestyle of faithfulness:

- **Surrendered Control:** I do not control the outcome of the things to which I give myself.
- **Surrendered Identity:** I am not what I accomplish. My identity is not tied to my results.
- **Surrendered Work Ethic:** I am not called to an unsustainable pace, so, if the pace required for the work is unhealthy, maybe the work isn't from the Lord.
- **Surrendered Purpose:** I pursue the things that are important to God, the things that reflect His heart in the work that I do.

This is a unilateral surrender, permeating every area of our lives. There is no aspect of our minds, possessions, and passions that remains untouched by our complete surrender to the Lord. In each domain of our existence, we hear the same resounding call:

1. **Accomplishment**
   "Why am I not accomplishing more?" *Be faithful.*
2. **Comparison**
   "Why am I not as far along as so-and-so?" *Be faithful.*
3. **Failure**
   "How will I ever get beyond this huge mistake I made?" *Be faithful.*

4. **Regret**

    "All these things are broken in my life, and they are my fault. How am I supposed to move forward?" *Be faithful.*

5. **Reputation**

    "I work really hard to maintain a positive reputation in my community, but I'm afraid one day it'll all come crashing down." *Be faithful.*

6. **Revenue Generation**

    "We have a solid plan in place, but I'm still not sure we'll hit our numbers for the year." *Be faithful.*

7. **Ministry**

    "My church isn't growing, people are leaving, and I've been betrayed . . . again." *Be faithful.*

8. **Parenting**

    "My kids won't listen to me. I tell them the same thing over and over." *Be faithful.*

9. **Marriage**

    "I'm working on our marriage. I'm trying to grow, but my spouse isn't. I'm not sure I can take this anymore." *Be faithful.*

Faithfulness is a daily commitment to diligent dependence: hard work surrendered to God for the results. The faithful leader leans in, works hard, and trusts all the results and outcomes to the Lord.

ONLY BE A BRANCH

In one of Jesus' most famous and masterful parables, He describes with beautiful simplicity what our relationship with Him and the Father is like: "I am the vine; you are the branches. Whoever abides in me and I in him, he it is that bears much fruit, for apart from me you can do nothing" (John 15:5).

Andrew Murray comments on these verses in his book *The True Vine: Meditations for a Month on John 15:1–16.*

> What a life would come to us if we only consented to be branches! Dear child of God, learn the lesson. You have but one thing to do: Only be a branch—nothing more, nothing less! Just be a branch; Christ will be the Vine that gives all. And the Husbandman, the mighty God, who made the Vine what it is, will as surely make the branch what it ought to be.³

I'm picturing all the "You had one job" memes. We have one job: be the branch.

I'm part of an amazing group called C12, where CEOs, business owners, and executives come together monthly for Christ-centered, curriculum-driven peer advisory. My friend Bob, who leads the C12 Business Forum I'm a member of, regularly asks the CEOs in our forum, "What is the branch's job?" Someone in the forum will eventually speak up, "Produce fruit." With a smirk on his face and a tone dripping with "Nuh-uh, not so fast," Bob then reminds us, "Is it not the job of the *Holy Spirit* to produce fruit in our lives?" (Galatians 5).

I remember how frequently in elementary school I would be upset when I was *sure* I had the right answer in math class, but the teacher wouldn't agree with me. I would sit back, confident that my teacher would arrive at the same conclusion I did after she finished doing all her work and completing her proofs and publicly crown me "King of Math Class." That never happened. Instead, after the teacher would reach her conclusion (which correctly disagreed with mine), I'd freak out, frantically review my work, and find a humbling error in my logic that proved me wrong. That's how I feel every time Bob asks this question about the branch's job.

If the job of the branch is not to produce fruit, *then what is its job?*

Simple.

Abide.

The branch's job is to abide in the Vine.

Abiding in God is confessing your unfruitfulness apart from Him, laboring to stay close to Christ, and trusting God will bring fruitfulness in His timing.

You are not meant to be the vine. You never were. Apart from the vine (the Son), you can do nothing. Faithful leaders are content to be only a branch. They feel no need to simultaneously be the branch *and* their own life-giving source. They say with the other branches, "If alone I abide, all my needs will be supplied."

Are you trying to be the vine? What does your prayer life reveal about your commitment to abiding?

Be faithful in your simple role: abide in Christ. He will do His work through us.

GOD MOVES IN A MYSTERIOUS WAY

A former pastor in my life loved the hymn "God Moves in a Mysterious Way," by William Cowper (1774). The lyrics hung in his office to remind him who is in control.

> God moves in a mysterious way
> His wonders to perform . . .
>
> Deep in unsearchable mines
> Of never-failing skill,
> He treasures up His bright designs
> And works His sovereign will . . .[4]

We can't look in the rearview mirror of our lives, find places with great results and say, "There was God." We also can't look in the mirror, see all the poor results, and ask, "Where was God?" We can't assume every good outcome is due to His blessing or that every poor outcome is due to His displeasure. We don't get to know why God wants our results to turn out the way He does. God's perfect plans will look like a mystery to us.

For me, I could not see how the robbery at PHOS was anything but wasted. I knew God would be good through the process, but I couldn't see how He would be good *in* the process. Until I started to watch.

I began looking for God at work as we walked through this situation with the detectives over the next few weeks. I watched as our friends, clients, and community united around us. I saw our team rally together like never before. People started showing up at the studio with snack bags, pizza parties, boxes of cookies, donuts, and gift cards. Over lunches, in text messages, and during meetings, people were praying for us, encouraging us, and reminding us that God was going to move in and through this.

One of our executive team members remarked, "I feel such a sense of community and really banding together." Another executive was out on vacation, heard about what was going on, and texted us, "I kind of feel like I am missing out, which is pretty awesome if you think about it."

Based on tattoos our cameras had captured on the suspect's arm, the detectives were able to identify the man and make an arrest. The state attorney permitted me to write a victim letter that was to be read at his sentencing. In the letter, I was able to extend forgiveness, share my own testimony, and offer the man an opportunity to start his relationship with Jesus. The story was picked up by a local pastor, and the letter was read in front of his church that weekend.

In the end, 90% of our things were returned, we had no measurable data loss, our cash position made it easy to purchase replacements, and we came out stronger as a team.

God didn't have to do any of those things to be good—nor did He have to explain His reasons for letting these things happen. In every moment of that story, God was in control, and His plan was good. Mysterious—but good.

Sometimes God's plan is for big results: Peter preached at Pentecost, and 3,000 people got saved.

Sometimes God's plan is no results: Paul preached in Lystra and was stoned into a bloody pulp and then dragged out of the city.

Peter was faithful and saw God do something huge.

Paul was faithful and almost died. Both pleased God.

Eventually, Paul's friends found him lying in the road. Acts 14 tells us the rest of the story,

> But when the disciples gathered about [Paul], he rose up and entered the city, and on the next day he went on with Barnabas to Derbe. When they had preached the gospel to that city and had made many disciples, they returned to Lystra and to Iconium and to Antioch, strengthening the souls of the disciples, encouraging them to continue in the faith, and saying that through many tribulations we must enter the kingdom of God. (Acts 14:20–22)

When the Jews left Paul in the street, he was so badly injured that they thought he was dead. Amazingly, the very next day he was preaching the gospel in Derbe. He then went back to Lystra, where he had just been stoned, eager to strengthen the believers there.

That is faithfulness.

It wasn't Paul's business to succeed. His business was simply to be faithful to do what God had called him to do and trust the mysterious plan of a good and faithful God. He got up, did the hard work again, and entrusted himself to a faithful God.

> Therefore let those who suffer according to God's will entrust their souls to a faithful Creator while doing good. (1 Peter 4:19)

The success of Paul's ministry wasn't based on whether or not he saw a huge crowd run to Jesus, but whether or not he faithfully continued to do good and entrust himself to a faithful God even in his suffering. That's our calling.

DEAD TO RESULTS

Outcome-based thinking stands in stark contrast to the faithfulness mindset.

What does it mean to be a successful parent, leader, pastor, or friend? It means you are faithful. It means that every day you get up and go after the hard things with God's strength, for the glory of God, fully surrendered to God's plan for your leadership with your kids, your business, your ministry, and yourself.

You are not what you accomplish.

You were never meant to be.

You are meant to be the branch.

Abide. Entrust yourself and your results to God. That's your job. Faithful leaders say over themselves,

> ***I am successful simply if I am faithful, regardless of whether I am effectual.***

We are to aim for great results and set our sights high because we know we serve an able and powerful God. We should echo the words of William Carey, "Expect great things from God; attempt great things for God."[5] But, we should always hold our plans with open hands in case God wants to redirect us. We should always stay dead to results and outcomes, knowing that God's plan may not be what we've always envisioned.

It is not your business to succeed. Instead, God is calling you to be faithful. He's calling you to be like Him.

3

THE ONE CALLED FAITHFUL AND TRUE

Then I saw heaven opened, and behold, a white horse! The one sitting on it is called Faithful and True.

REVELATION 19:11

SHELLEY AND I are scuba divers. It's actually one of the things that initially drew us together, as it is a rare thing for two high schoolers to meet and have a mutual love for scuba diving.

My wife loves to dive in the ocean, but I can get very, very seasick. (Plus, I don't like salt water. Don't get me started.) To compromise, we mostly dive in freshwater springs.

We live next to one of the spring diving capitals of the world, famous for its underground cave system. While we don't have a desire to complete a cave certification, I was able to convince Shelley to complete a cavern certification with me. Unlike in cave diving, when cavern diving, you must never be more than 200 feet from the surface, and you must still be able to see ambient light somewhere in the cavern with your light off.

One of the most thrilling experiences in cavern diving is attempting to enter a spring's mouth where the water comes out of the cavern.

Ginnie Springs is a local second-magnitude spring, meaning that the spring puts out 37.6 million gallons of water flow every day, or 435 gallons of water per second. Compare that to a fire hydrant's 8 gallons per second, and you can begin to imagine the amount of water we are talking about.

When diving down to enter a cavern and nearing its mouth, you begin to feel the force of the water's flow. Most of the time, the only way you'll make it into the cavern is by grabbing on to the rocks lining the cavern's mouth and slowly pulling yourself inward rock by rock. At that point, the pressure of the water is causing your cheeks to flap violently in the water, your hair is flying straight back, and your fingers are gripping tightly just to hang on.

That overpowering, torrential force of water is the image presented of God's faithfulness in Exodus 34.

> The LORD, the LORD, a God merciful and gracious, slow to anger, and *abounding* in steadfast love and faithfulness. (Exodus 34:6, emphasis mine)

Like the mouth of a spring, the character of God is abounding, overflowing, and bursting with faithfulness. Everything God does is done with faithfulness. He could not act any other way:

> For the word of the LORD is upright, and all his work is done in faithfulness. (Psalm 33:4)

> I will not remove from him my steadfast love or be false to my faithfulness. (Psalm 89:33)

There are few things I rejoice over more than the faithfulness of God toward me. So many times, reflecting on the faithfulness of God has brought me to tears and caused hope to flood into the broken places of my heart. When I'm not sure if God loves me anymore, when I don't know if He'll forgive me, when I'm unsure I can trust Him to come through, when I don't know how

I'm going to make it through, when it feels like He's abandoned me—I know I can trust His faithfulness.

A verse I read recently took God's faithfulness to a whole new level for me and taught me something about God I had never seen before. John says in Revelation 19:11, "Then I saw heaven opened, and behold, a white horse! The one sitting on it is called Faithful and True."

God not only *acts* with faithfulness but He is also the One *called* Faithful, just as much as He is called True.

The One called Faithful calls *us* to be faithful.

As we pursue this calling, the most fruitful way for us to be conformed to this image is to look at God. As we look at His faithfulness, we'll see the areas of our lives in which we need to grow in faithfulness.

How does God demonstrate His faithfulness to us? The faithfulness of God is displayed in His love, forgiveness, promises, provision, and jealousy.

UNREQUITED LOVE

The most moving cinematic representation of God's love I've ever seen was a short film about a train track manager and his son.

In the video, we see the father positioned at a lift station near a train bridge spanning a waterway, while his son enjoys some fishing by the water. The father affectionately watches over his son and operates the mechanism to raise the tracks on the bridge, creating ample space for a large boat to sail underneath.

As the boat passes, the father attends to some needs in the station house, when the son hears the sound of a train off in the distance headed for the bridge. But the bridge is still lifted.

The father had previously shown his son a red lever he could manually pull on the bridge to lower the tracks if there was ever an emergency, so the boy abandons his fishing gear and runs toward the bridge.

Eventually, the father also hears the train's horn. He looks down from the operating station and sees his son lying on the tracks, trying to reach for the red lever.

The father starts shouting urgently, calling out to his son to move and get out of harm's way. But as the son reaches out for the lever with a long stretch, he misses and tumbles into a space where the draw bridge will crush him if closed. The dad begins to panic.

Frantically, he starts doing the math in his head: if he runs to rescue his son, he can't lower the bridge, and everyone on the train will die. But if he lowers the bridge to keep everyone on the train alive, his son will die.

The father is seen crying, waiting, screaming, and pacing until the last second, when he chooses to lower the bridge, crushing his son.

He rushes downstairs and onto the platform just as the train begins to glide past. The expression of horror etched on his face, the tears streaming down his cheeks, and his anguished screams create a haunting scene.

As the train passes by, we get several glimpses into the train cars and the lives of its passengers. While the father is outside wailing, the people inside are oblivious. They're shooting up drugs, kissing, and arguing with one another—completely unaware of the sacrificial love that was just poured out for them.[6]

That's unrequited love.

Because God is faithful, the undeserving are shown love. The loveless are shown kindness. Spiritual enemies are saved from destruction and called sons and daughters.

> The Lord favors those who fear Him,
> Those who wait for His faithfulness. (Psalm 147:11, NASB)

Look to the cross and see a God who selflessly sacrificed everything for your sake. See a Father who, despite the shortcomings in your reciprocation of love, abundantly pours out His own faithful love for you.

God's faithfulness, displayed in unrequited love, silences fears that whisper "I'm not sure if God loves me anymore."

UNCEASING FORGIVENESS

The word *omniscience* is a theological term that refers to God being all-knowing. It is a compound of two Latin words: *omnis*, meaning "all" or "everything," and *scientia*, meaning "knowledge." God knows everything at all times.[7] Nothing escapes His complete comprehension. There is nothing beyond God's understanding.

God knows your thoughts before you think them, He knew you before you were conceived, and He searches the depths of your heart to understand even the motives and intentions of every choice you make.

Yet here lies a profound mystery: this all-knowing God also intentionally chooses to forget.

> For I will be merciful toward their iniquities, and I will remember their sins no more. (Hebrews 8:12)

The all-knowing God chooses not to remember our sins. He knows them and chooses to forget them. **Every unfaithful decision we make finds forgiveness in God's faithful love.**

> If we confess our sins, he is *faithful* and just to forgive us our sins and to cleanse us from all unrighteousness. (1 John 1:9, emphasis mine)

In Jesus, our sins have been blotted out (Isaiah 43:25). In Jesus, our sins have been removed as far as the east is from the west (Psalm 103:12). In Jesus, our sins have been cast behind God's back (Isaiah 38:17). He has forgotten them.

It is impossible for God to hold your sins against you any longer, because He canceled the record of debt that stood against you (Colossians 2:14). Jesus took the record of your sins that He could have used to indict you before the Father, and He shredded it to pieces. Corrie ten Boom, a Christian Holocaust survivor, says that our sins have been "cast into the deepest sea and a sign [has been] put up that says NO FISHING ALLOWED."[8]

You cannot be punished for sins that Jesus has already paid the debt for.

The faithfulness of God did that for you.

God's faithfulness, displayed in unceasing forgiveness, silences fears that whisper "I'm not sure if God will forgive me."

UNBROKEN PROMISES

Just as we can trust the omniscient God will remember our sins no more, we can know that all His promises find their "yes" in Jesus (2 Corinthians 1:20). God has never spoken anything He was not fully committed to seeing through to perfect completion.

Joshua, one of the leaders of ancient Israel, was warning and charging his people when he reminded them of this:

> You know in your hearts and souls, all of you, that not one word has failed of all the good things that the LORD your God promised concerning you. All have come to pass for you; not one of them has failed. (Joshua 23:14)

Without fail, God will bring to fruition every promise He has ever made to us, whether it has already been accomplished or is yet to be. It is impossible for Him to do otherwise, as His very nature compels Him to fulfill every promise He has uttered.

One of the challenges we encounter as we strive to trust this truth is that God surpasses our limited perspective because He operates on timelines different from our own.

Early in Jewish history, God promises an important man named Abraham that He is going to build a nation through him and his descendants. But when Abraham and his wife Sarah still don't have a child by the time she is 90 years old (you read that right), they are both scratching their heads, thinking, *Yeah, about that* . . .

God was faithful to His promise, and, eventually, Abraham and Sarah had a son. Generations later, his offspring would become the bedrock of the entire nation of Israel and give birth to the Messiah, the ultimate embodiment of God's faithful commitment to His promises.

God is famous for eleventh-hour, clutch saves. And, whatever promises we don't see fulfilled in this lifetime, we'll see brought to completion in our life to come.

For Good Friday one year, my wife and I designed a beautiful textural art piece for our church's stage. It took several months, but we handwove 1,200 feet of thick, chunky red yarn together to create a long braid. We hung the braid over a cross on the stage, carried it down the stairs, through the sanctuary, out into the foyer, then attached it to the front door of the church, symbolizing that the faithfulness of God displayed on the cross follows us everywhere we go.

We also designed a two-sided postcard with some blanks to fill in. On the front, a prompt read, "LOOKING BACK—The One who was faithful unto death *has been* faithful in my . . ." We encouraged the church to think about different areas of their lives where God had been faithful to them in the past (e.g., their marriage, business, parenting, etc.) and write them down on the blank lines.

On the back, the prompt read, "LOOKING FORWARD—The One who was faithful unto death *will be* faithful in my . . ." Here, we encouraged everyone to write down the areas of their lives where they needed God to be faithful in the future.

I was so busy that night leading worship that I didn't get to fill out one of the cards until Sunday morning.

Honestly, I should have seen the problem with the cards so much sooner.

The first part was easy to fill out: *I've seen you be faithful with my wife, my children, etc.* But, as I went to fill out the other side, I realized something that should have been so obvious during our planning process for this special service element. All the places I need God to be faithful in my life moving forward are all the same places I've *already* seen Him be faithful in the past.

I need You to faithfully lead my business. *You always have.*

I need You to faithfully care for my family. *You always have.*

I need You to faithfully guide my ministry. *You always have.*

Our hope for God's future faithfulness is His spotless historical record. There has never been a promise He has not, or will not in the future, see to completion. The One who has been trustworthy will be trustworthy tomorrow, the day after that, and into eternity.

> He delivered us from such a deadly peril, *and he will deliver us.* On him we have set our hope that *he will deliver us again.* (2 Corinthians 1:10, emphasis mine)

God's faithfulness, displayed in unbroken promises, silences fears that whisper "I'm not sure if God will come through."

UNDESERVED PROVISION

In 2020, when COVID-19 impacted every economic sector, I immediately pivoted my personal growth strategy. Knowing that I had never faced anything like the season I was about to enter, I signed up for every webinar I could find about leadership in the middle of a crisis. I still have a note on my phone titled "Crisis Leadership Webinars," where I collected my notes from every session I attended.

In a Michael Hyatt webinar, he shared this simple, encouraging thought, "You have survived 100% of every crisis you've faced. How do I know that? Because you're here right now."

Every need we've ever had has been met. Every single one.

The crazy part is that you didn't do anything to warrant those provisions. You couldn't have. There are not enough good, kind, loving, or godly things you could have done that would have twisted God's arm behind His back until He shouted, "Uncle! I'll give you what you need!" He knows your needs and faithfully provides your daily bread simply because He desires to.

God is always faithful to meet our physical needs:

> And my God will supply every need of yours according to his riches in glory in Christ Jesus. (Philippians 4:19)

In moments of temptation, God is faithful to provide a way out:

> No temptation has overtaken you that is not common to man. God is faithful, and he will not let you be tempted beyond your ability, but with the temptation he will also provide the way of escape, that you may be able to endure it. (1 Corinthians 10:13)

In moments of spiritual battle, God is faithful to be our shield:

> But the Lord is faithful. He will establish you and guard you against the evil one. (2 Thessalonians 3:3)

What do you have that you did not receive?

Nothing and no one can do anything to you about which the Lord, in His faithfulness and His goodness, has not said, "I permit this for My glory and your good."

Worry, anxiety, and fear are the enemy's tools for disrupting the peace that comes from this truth:

> He will cover you with his pinions, and under his wings you will find refuge; his faithfulness is a shield and buckler. (Psalm 91:4)

God's faithfulness is a giant, impenetrable shield surrounding you. When cancer strikes, your account overdrafts, or your pregnancy fails, you have a sure and steady anchor. We sing with Edward Mote, "When all around my soul gives way, He then is all my hope and stay."[9] The greatest thing God can provide for us is Himself, and He has promised to provide that in every season. He is our hope and stay, and His faithfulness will provide for every need we have.

God's faithfulness, displayed in undeserved provision, silences fears that whisper "I'm not sure how we'll get through this."

UNRELENTING JEALOUSY

It's easy for me to give up on people. When they fail me or disappoint me, it is far easier than it should be for me to simply say, "You're dead to me." It's hard to keep loving people.

I'm grateful Jesus doesn't give up on people like I have.

He doesn't walk away.

He doesn't stop going after His people.

He doesn't give up on people who wander.

The Bible uses the term *jealous* to describe God's heart. His jealousy is a relentless commitment to the good of His people, an intense care for their protection, and an endless pursuit of their well-being that compels Him to go to great lengths to draw back in the stragglers and go after the drifters.

The faithful jealousy of God is seen in the way He leads His children without fail.

> "My son, do not regard lightly the discipline of the Lord, nor be weary when reproved by him. For the Lord disciplines the one he loves, and chastises every son whom he receives." . . . God is treating you as sons. For what son is there whom his father does not discipline? (Hebrews 12:5–7)

Because God is jealous over us, wanting us to be near Him and like Him, He disciplines us. He corrects us, even when that correction is painful. That's what a faithful, loving father does. He doesn't let His children just walk away; He goes after them.

Why? Because **God cares more about making us like Him than about making us comfortable**.

How can that mindset shape our leadership in the office or at home?

God's faithfulness, displayed in unrelenting jealousy, silences fears that whisper "I'm not sure if God has abandoned me."

CONSIDER HIM FAITHFUL

Centuries after Sarah finally gave birth to her son, Isaac, the writers of the New Testament would speak of her faithfulness:

> By faith Sarah herself received power to conceive, even when she was past the age, since she *considered him faithful* who had promised. (Hebrews 11:11, emphasis mine)

Sarah received the power to conceive by faith because she considered God to be faithful. She knew something about God that persuaded her to put her faith in Him.

What would you believe by faith if you considered God to be faithful?

The outcome-based mindset can threaten our surety in God's faithfulness. When we don't get the results or outcomes we want from God, we can be tempted to think, *See! God's not listening, and He's not trustworthy*. But we're so wrong. We must not measure God's faithfulness by our desired outcomes or subordinate our trust in God's faithfulness to our desired results. He is faithful regardless of our outcomes, and we must trust Him in spite of what our circumstances may tempt us to conclude.

In fact, God is faithful and wise and good in ways we cannot even fathom. Like the overwhelming force of water I feel when I dive to a submerged cave, God's faithfulness springs from depths unimaginable:

> Oh, the depth of the riches and wisdom and knowledge of God! How unsearchable are his judgments and how inscrutable his ways! "For who has known the mind of the Lord, or who has been his counselor?" (Romans 11:33–34)

God's ways are not our own, and, because God doesn't think like us, you can't predict *what* He will do. You can, however, predict *how* He will act because you can know the heart of God. You can know what He values, and you can learn more about how He thinks. God's faithfulness assures that what we have seen will be repeated and what has been forecast for the future will assuredly come to pass.

Here's what we know about the One called Faithful and True:

He loves us even when we don't return it.

He forgives us even when we haven't earned it.

He fulfills His promise even when we've struggled to believe it.

He provides for us even though we'll never deserve it.

He longs for us jealously even though we aren't worthy of it.

Maybe it's been a while since you've looked closely at this aspect of God's character. Maybe you've lost sight of the wonder of God and the gospel, and your heart has become cold to the beauty of God. Maybe you've become myopic, focusing only on the day-to-day, the size of your to-do list, and the unending pressures of managing teams and running an organization.

I get it. I've been there many times.

Faithfulness calls us to focus beyond the immediate and to consider and be transformed by the eternal.

The One called Faithful and True hasn't given up on you. He hasn't thrown in the towel. Our faithful God is calling you: "Come back. I'm still here. I love you."

4

THE DAILY HARD WORK OF FAITHFULNESS

We battle the false promises of the world with better promises from God.
JOHN PIPER

OUR UNDERSTANDING OF the word *faithful* usually falls into one of two categories.

Sometimes we use this word simply to mean that someone is "full of faith." This is consistent with the Greek word in the Bible that we translate into English as *faithful*. The Greek word is simply an adjectival form of the word *faith*,[10] meaning the person we apply it to is "faith-y, or trust-y." When we call someone faithful, we are communicating that this person has a great trust and confidence in God.

Usually, though, when we use the word *faithful*, we use it to describe someone's behavior, not just their belief. When we say, "He is a faithful husband," we mean that he hasn't cheated on his wife (behavior), not that he trusts God and his wife (belief).

As a result, embedded within the word *faithful* is a dynamic interplay between our convictions and conduct. Faithfulness is equal parts belief and behavior, trust and obedience, resting in God and working for Him. Understanding the word *faithful* in this way confirms our description of *faithfulness* from chapter 2:

Faithfulness is daily hard work entrusted to God.

Because faithfulness is a fruit of the Spirit (Galatians 5:22–23), there is truth to the idea that faithfulness is a uniquely Christian attribute—one that Christ wants us to exhibit as we grow spiritually. To truly exhibit faithfulness, our conduct must reflect a conviction about God—namely, that He is faithful and calls *us* to be faithful.

As we daily walk with God, we abide in the vine (Jesus), and we (the branches) bear spiritual fruit, including faithfulness. This belief-driven, behavior-focused calling to be faithful should bud and sprout in every offshoot of our lives:

Our business(es)

Our leadership

Our marriage

Our parenting

Our relationship with Jesus

Our relationships with friends and family

Our church (ministry)

Our local and global community (missions)

That's a lot of areas in which we are called to be faithful.

It's a lot because faithfulness involves everything every day. Public and private, faithfulness is a call to all that we think, say, do, and desire. This is the daily hard work of faithfulness.

FAITHFUL IN THE SMALL THINGS

Our calling to be faithful begins in the small things: the mundane, daily work we find ourselves doing.

Jesus spoke to this when He said,

> One who is faithful in a very little is also faithful in much, and one who is dishonest in a very little is also dishonest in much. If then you have not been faithful in the unrighteous wealth, who will entrust to you the true riches? (Luke 16:10–11)

Jesus is saying, "You want a lot? Be faithful with a little. Be faithful with the things I've already given you." Instead of driving for more and more, Jesus wants us to be faithful in the little that we already have.

Ambition drives us to want more. We look at people who have a lot of influence, authority, power, money, and fame, and we think, *I could do that. In fact, if I were in their shoes, I'd do it better.*

There are so many times I've thought *I'm ready for more, Lord. Now is the time. Send the next big thing my way.* But I wasn't ready (emotionally, spiritually, or professionally), and the Lord knew that.

It's a blessing that the Lord doesn't answer every prayer we pray.

I am regularly counseling business leaders who are so excited and proud to share about all their successes. They love to boast of the number of employees they have, their year-over-year growth figures, and their expanded annual earnings. But when we get past the vanity metrics and start talking about things that matter, it's clear that, behind the scenes, they are completely broken. Their emotional, mental, and spiritual health is in shambles, their business is held together with sticks and gum, their marriage is on the rocks, and their kids are—wait, what kids?

These business leaders are living proof that having "much" does not satisfy—and can be a torment—when we have yet to prove faithful with the "little"

God has given us. And the "little" He has given us may be a lot more than we realize, if we look at the whole picture.

For example, we want more for the organizations we lead (more clients, more opportunities, more results), but what about our homes? Are we being faithful behind closed doors in our marriage, parenting, and other relationships that are close to God's heart? Hear this from Dorothy Kelley Patterson:

> Busyness is not godliness. God is not impressed with your production capacity as much as He is concerned that the product of your home—your own children—be chiseled and molded and perfected to the best of your ability. You may tire of this mundane task, but the Lord admonishes you not to grow weary and promises to supply the energy and strength as needed in this all-important task (Isa. 40:28–31). God's strength is for what He plans for you to do—not stamina for everything you might want to do![11]

Our nature is to want more things—but what if we simply wanted more for the things we already have? God wants us to concentrate on being faithful with the things He has already given us—not on imagining how faithful we might be if only He would give us more.

What if all you have right now is all you'll ever have? What if your bank account's balance is the highest it will ever get, your position is the highest in the company it will ever be, your salary is the highest you will ever receive, and your position of influence is the biggest it will ever reach? Could you be content and faithful for the rest of your life with what you have at this point in your life?

You don't need more to be faithful. You can be faithful right here, right now, with what you have at this moment. And growing in faithfulness lies in the little, simple, daily choices that we make to move in that direction.

Want to be a better spouse? Do something different today, something small, to move in that direction. Send an unexpected love text, perform an unprompted act of service, give an unrequested shoulder massage, deliver a bouquet of flowers, sit down on the couch and draw your spouse out with questions, or joyfully volunteer to do your spouse's favorite thing together even if you don't like doing it.

Want to be a better parent? Do something different today, something small, to move in that direction. Let your kids know you're proud of them, give them extra long hugs, ask if you can help with their homework, play a board game with them (and stay off your phone while doing so), or go pray with them before bed.

Want to be a better leader? Do something different today, something small, to move in that direction. Call someone on your team who is struggling and ask them if you can pray for them, don't be late (even by a minute) to a single meeting, spend an extra 15 to 30 minutes preparing for your review with a key subordinate so you can be specific about ways his or her work is helping your organization fulfill its mission, or go deal with the difficult customer you've been avoiding at all costs.

These aren't extravagant asks. They are simple opportunities for you to be faithful in the small things. Any one of these small acts will move you toward increased levels of faithfulness in your marriage, parenting, and organization.

Faithful leaders don't make huge, outlandish, and impulsive commitments that they'll never see through to the end. They make small, sensible commitments that they diligently work toward fulfilling.

It's not reasonable for you to walk into work and shout, "That's it! We are changing everything! For the past few months, I've been slacking about some key initiatives, and we are going to double down—nay, triple down—on our efforts!" It would be too much. Two weeks later, you wouldn't be doing a single thing you committed to during this frantic, "corrective" leadership moment. And your lack of integrity in completing those initiatives would erode your team's trust in you and perpetuate your unfaithfulness.

A great practical book on changing your habits is *Atomic Habits*, by James Clear. Clear encourages us to aim to get better each day by 1%. That's it. It seems so small, but if we got 1% better daily for one year, we'd be 37 times better than when we started (1% compounded over 365 days is a 3,700% increase). But if we truly want to change, Clear says, we must first examine ourselves:

> Your actions reveal how badly you want something. If you keep saying something is a priority but you never act on it, then you don't really want it. It's time to have an honest conversation with yourself. Your actions reveal your true motivations.[12]

You can say you want to be better, but if you don't work toward that 1% of improvement each day, you'll never change (because you don't really want to). The daily hard work of faithfulness is asking, "What small things am I called to be faithful with today?" Then take the next small step. The road to faithfulness in *much* starts with daily faithfulness in *little* and it starts where you are right now: wherever God has placed you, or, if you prefer, planted you.

WHERE YOU'RE PLANTED

The outcome-based mindset loves to whisper to us, "Unless you are a part of something big, it's not worth doing. Your impact is too small. Bigger is always better."

I saw a post on a worship leader forum I'm a part of, in which the author shared,

> I was serving at a church of 900+ people, and now I serve at a church of approximately 300 people. Upon learning that I serve at a smaller church, a person who serves at a larger church told me, "I'm glad you're continuing to serve, *just don't get stuck*." (emphasis mine)

Is everyone who serves at a small church, leads a small team, or runs a small business "stuck"?

Faithfulness is size-independent.

I served the first church I was seriously committed to as a believer for more than 10 years. When I eventually started attending a new church, it was almost eight times the size of my first church. I didn't feel any more fulfilled in that ministry. Size is a vanity metric that plays no role in your faithfulness. You could be faithful or unfaithful in a tiny, small, large, or giant context.

FAITHFULNESS VERSUS LOYALTY

Being faithful where you're planted doesn't always mean you're supposed to stay where you are. God may choose to uproot you and plant you somewhere else. One area I have had to grow in pertaining to leadership is seeing people leave PHOS.

I remember a time when a great employee we had recently hired entered my office to give me the typical "I wasn't looking. . . . An opportunity popped up. . . . I can't say no" speech.

I thanked him for letting me know, honored the work he'd done, and dismissed him from my office.

As I closed the door behind him, I stumbled backward and slowly rolled down onto the floor. I was crushed. I had invested so much in him, so much was riding on his employment, and I felt betrayed. For 15 minutes, I was sprawled on my office carpet, weeping silently and pretending not to hear the repeated knocks and the voices asking, "Brandon, are you in there?"

For many years, I didn't handle people leaving very well. In a small organization, it's easy to think, *How could you abandon me?*

What I've had to realize is that **faithfulness is not the same thing as loyalty**.

I love loyalty. I think it's one of my personal core values (which probably plays into the pain of people departing). Loyalty is being highly committed to someone or something. It is an allegiance to a person, cause, or ideal that causes us to stick around. It is usually driven by strong feelings of trust or duty.

Feelings of loyalty, though, can even cause people to remain in situations that are threatening, inappropriate, or harmful.

Faithfulness, on the other hand, isn't just about *remaining*; it's about *pursuing* God and living open-handedly before Him every day.

The question I have had to increasingly check myself with is, "What if being faithful to your calling meant you had to say no to your loyalty?" That was my former employee's story. Yet for years, my personal valuing of loyalty blinded me from seeing that being faithful to the Lord may spark a realignment of a person's loyalties, especially at work.

Dr. Henry Cloud, in his book *Necessary Endings*, lays out three steps to navigate the faithfulness/loyalty relationship:[13]

1. Do the absolute best you can in every season you're in. (Loyalty and Faithfulness)
2. Be bold and courageous to end things and move to the next season when it comes. (Faithfulness)
3. Return to step one. (Faithfulness)

The daily hard work of faithfulness tells us to work hard where we've been planted. Faithfulness doesn't mean we can't leave or shouldn't leave certain circumstances, but it rejects the idea that the place where you are called must be bigger and better for you to be happy and fulfilled. Be faithful where God has planted you until He transplants you somewhere else.

FEELINGS AND FAITHFULNESS

Faithfulness is not driven by feelings. Most of the time, our commitment to faithfulness means we move forward *in spite of* our feelings.

John Piper is probably the most consistently impactful author and speaker in my life. His magnum opus is a book called *Desiring God*, 360 pages of

God-centered, Bible-saturated material about why and how our deepest happiness and joy can be found only in Jesus. It's refreshing and so challenging.

What I really love, though, is his subsequent book *When I Don't Desire God: How to Fight for Joy*. That's real life. Piper is saying, "Hey, Christian, you should desire God . . . but here's how to fight for that if you're not currently feeling it."

After church one Sunday, I asked one of my worship team members how his devotional time was with the Lord, and he responded, "It doesn't feel natural. It feels like a discipline."

"Is anything spiritual supposed to feel natural?" I asked him. "Our natural inclination is to oppose and reject God, to run away from Him. That's what feels the most natural in our lives."

Everything spiritual in your life is a discipline. Training yourself to desire spiritual things is part of how you "put off your old self, which belongs to your former manner of life and is corrupt through deceitful desires . . . to be renewed in the spirit of your minds, and to put on the new self, created after the likeness of God in true righteousness and holiness" (Ephesians 4:22–24).

In their song "Waiting Room," Shane and Shane put it this way, "Lord, I know if I change my mind / You will change my heart in time."[14] That is faithful leadership. Though I don't feel it, I will choose it. Though I don't want it, I will commit to it. And, as I do so, I believe that you'll change my heart. The psalmist says,

> I have *chosen* the way of faithfulness; I set your rules before me.
> (Psalm 119:30, emphasis mine)

Faithful leadership is something we choose, regardless of feelings, because we desire to honor the Lord with the way we live and lead.

Often, we excuse our unfaithful behavior by saying, "I chose not to do the right thing because I didn't want to be fake. I didn't feel like doing it, so I didn't want to be disingenuous by doing it. That would have been wrong." What this usually boils down to, though, is *I didn't want to do the right thing, so I didn't.*

That is the opposite of the psalmist "choos[ing] the way of faithfulness."

The truth is, the only time we are faking is when we're doing something we'd rather not be doing and deceitfully tell someone, "I really want to be doing this." **When we choose to do the thing we are called to even when we don't want to do it, we are choosing faithfulness.**

One of my pastors once told me, "Feelings should be the caboose of the train, not the engine." Feelings can't drive the train, but if we are faithful, they will eventually follow. Change your behavior, and change your mind, and God will change your heart in time.

Jerry Bridges puts this idea another way, writing, "We must not allow our emotions to hold sway over our minds. Rather, we must seek to let the truth of God rule our minds. Our emotions must become subservient to the truth."[15]

Even Jesus, who was subjected to the same temptations as we are (yet resisted them), had to subordinate His emotions to His Father's calling. The night before His crucifixion, Jesus' soul was troubled and He was in agony over the suffering that awaited Him at the cross (Luke 22:44; John 12:27). He asked His Father to take it from Him (Luke 22:42). But, despite how Jesus *felt*, He was faithful to the end. And, if it weren't for Christ's faithfulness, we would still be dead in our sins.

Feelings cannot be the determining factor for our actions. If we wait until we feel like doing something or until inspiration hits, we'll miss out on loads of opportunities to create, inspire, and serve others. Shola Richards, founder and CEO of Go Together Global, once shared, "Commitment is doing what you said you were going to do long after the mood you said it in has left you."[16]

Long after you've made a commitment, faithfulness requires you to ask:

>Is this commitment still important (and binding)?

If it is, why am I hesitating to go and do it?

If it isn't, why am I hesitating to change or remove it?

The daily hard work of faithfulness requires us to do the things we don't always feel like doing and to lean into the painful, hard-to-swallow moments of life and leadership. Be faithful, and your feelings will follow.

BE THE BUFFALO

In the open flatlands of the western United States, a storm can be seen from miles away. With few trees to obstruct the view, you can get a long visual lead time on dark clouds forming and heading toward your location. When a herd of cattle sees the storm headed their way, they run from it.

Buffalo, on the other hand, group together and charge straight at the storm. When the storm hits, cows end up spending more time in it because of their attempt at avoidance, while the buffalo spend *less* time in it because of their choice to face it. That's the buffalo mindset.[17] That's the heartbeat of a faithful leader committed to persevering in the hard things.

Faithful leaders run right at a storm. They embrace the daily demands and difficult tasks, tackling them directly without hesitation. Their unwavering commitment to taking on the tough items of the day allows them to navigate challenges more efficiently, spending less time in the chaos of uncertainties.

Faithful leader, you can't shy away from the hard things. Get your team together and courageously run straight toward the storms. It is not faithful leadership for you to avoid hard conversations because you want to be "loving" to people. It is, in fact, unloving to avoid telling people the hard truth.

Do the daily hard work of faithfulness and lead your people toward the hard stuff in life. Be a buffalo leader.

MORE THAN MAKING STUFF OUT OF STEEL

The PHOS team once hosted a strategic planning session for a manufacturing client at a local Italian restaurant. The client had been in business for more than 50 years and was a few years into third-generation leadership within the organization. After starting in the garage of the founder's house, the company was now internationally known for crafting custom vacuum chambers for researchers, scientists, and engineers.

With their key leadership team gathered, a few members of the PHOS team present, and some homemade plates of lasagna begging to be eaten, we dug into the meal and into a conversation about the company's purpose and mission.

I started the meeting by referencing a few key notes about the business that I had written down beforehand, using a giant notepad propped against the back of a chair as my presentation board. In my own words, I summarized the core services of the client's company, then dove into the meeting's key question (while I took a bite of the still-hot Italian classic): "Given the clarity we have about what you do, tonight we want to talk about why you do what you do. So, tell me: what is your company's *why*? Why do you do what you do?"

Crickets.

Typical.

Finally, one brave soul was willing to pipe up, "It's not sexy. We just make stuff out of steel."

"Okay," I responded. Understanding this process usually takes some digging, I continued. "But why? Why is doing that important?"

Another silence.

An even braver soul offered some insight into the level of trust present within the organization: "We do what we do so we can support the lifestyle of the leadership team."

Ouch! My heart sank into my lasagna on that one. I wondered if I was going to be able to recover the meeting.

"Wow, okay . . ." I said, trying to direct the conversation back to the topic at hand. "That aside, why do you *personally* come to work?"

"Because I only live half a mile from work, and I can walk there each morning!" shared a new participant enthusiastically.

On the inside, I was now banging my head against a closed fist.

Then something happened in the meeting I'll never forget.

Resolved to get the answer I wanted, I asked again, "Okay, but why is coming to work important? Why is doing what you do important? When you're home for Christmas and your mom or dad asks again about what you do, what do you tell them?"

After no small amount of time, someone right next to me spoke up, "You know, I was talking to one of our welders once, and I told him that the piece he was creating was going to a cancer research lab, and I saw his face light up."

Bingo.

"Yeah," replied another quickly around the table, "when my mom and I are driving on the interstate and we pass the billboard with the picture of the Large Hadron Collider, I point at it and tell my mom, 'that's what we do!'"

Now the room was on fire.

For several minutes, I sat back in my chair, listening to stories of the company's impact on various market sectors, including science, technology, and health, and I thought to myself, *Job complete*.

They say the longest journey in the world is the 18 inches between your head and your heart. That evening, those two things got connected for the leaders of that business.

Maybe for the first time in the history of that company, the light bulb went on that their daily mission was about more than just making stuff out of steel.

When they build vacuum chambers, they help to find a cure for cancer, develop the next medical breakthrough, or engineer the next technological marvel.

For most of us, the vast majority of what we do in life is not sexy. Our daily grind isn't glamorous or newsworthy—it's just making stuff out of steel. But faithful leaders don't need things to glitter for their work to produce gladness. Faithful leaders find meaning in the mundane, knowing that their faithfulness in their daily hard work pleases the Lord. They know that behind the simple things we do is an eternal mission, a purpose, and an impact worth our faithfulness.

When we are able to make the connection between our head and our heart, the things we do and our *why*, the daily grind and our destiny, we find the power to lean into our work with purpose, be faithful, and finish well.

There is purpose in your work beyond the things you do. Have you taken the time to find it?

CHARACTER OVER CONTRIBUTION

In my own exploration of the outcome-based mindset, I find in myself a fear, not just of failure but of the shame of failure. My fears come not only from the thought of not completing my goals, reaching my dreams, accomplishing something grand, or living up to my potential but also from the shame of having to live on the other side of that "failure."

At a conference on the topic of purpose, one speaker used an illustration about the "Soul-Sucking CEO," the leader of Fear Incorporated.[18] As I listened to him describe this person's leadership style, I wrote in my journal, "You have been living and leading from a place of fear." I was looking over the past six months of my leadership and saw how fear and shame had driven negative leadership behaviors and habits.

The outcome-based mindset can drive so much fear:

Fear that my business is going to come crumbling down.

Fear that I'm going to lose my best people or my best client.

Fear that my reputation and influence will dry up.

Fear that I'm not enough.

The fear of shame kicks in when we start thinking, *Who would I be if I wasn't this or that person anymore?*

The overarching fear of the outcome-based mindset is the contribution failure: "I didn't give, do, or accomplish enough."

The psalmist also struggled with a fear of failure and shame. But, the psalmist's fear came from a concern over character failure, not contribution failure.

> Oh that my ways may be steadfast in keeping your statutes! Then I shall not be put to shame, having my eyes fixed on all your commandments. (Psalm 119:5–6)

The daily hard work of faithfulness calls us to define success differently, but it also calls us to define failure differently. For the faithful leader, failure isn't about a miss in outcomes but a miss in conduct. It's not about failing to see the fruits of our labor but failing to see the fruits of the Spirit.

Faithfulness is calling us to grow, to pursue the hard work of character transformation in our relationship with Jesus, and to see that pursuit as more valuable than results we may or may not produce.

Faithful leader, the best thing you can offer the people around you is a life lived for Christ. Shift what you fear and let God drive your identity and priorities.

TAKE THE NEXT STEP

During a training course with the pastoral team at my church, I was given a homework assignment that I had to complete with my wife. I was told that I needed to record her answer to this question word for word.

On a scale of 1–10 (1 being "I think you are the devil" and 10 being "I'm confused. Are you Jesus?"), how am I doing as a servant in our relationship?"

Shelley rated me a 4.

According to the scale, a 4 is more like Satan than Jesus.

That night, I handled the rating pretty well, but the next day it caused a big fight. For a week, I was upset, disappointed, and frustrated at the 4. I didn't like being scored that low. I didn't like the thought of walking into our next training session and having to talk through a 4.

I was upset because I saw the rating (outcome) as my identity.

What I needed to do was focus more on the homework assignment's second question:

What is one practical thing I could change to go up just one point in your mind?

The mission statement of the church I attend is "to help people take their next step with Jesus." What I love about this mission statement is that it can apply to any person we meet. It doesn't presuppose anything about someone's relationship with Jesus. We can simply work to identify where they need to take their next step with Jesus, then help them take it.

What I missed in that moment with Shelley was the most important part of the homework assignment: what do I need to do next to grow? What is my next step with Jesus?

Faithfulness isn't about scoring tens every day. Faithfulness is about taking your next step.

I don't want my wife to have to settle for who I am. But, by God's grace, she doesn't have to. I can choose to do the daily hard work of leaning into Jesus and working faithfully on one practical thing I can do to score just one point higher.

What is your next step toward faithfulness in your marriage, parenting, church, business, or community? Be faithful. Go and take it.

WILL TO BE FAITHFUL

In interviews with "successful" leaders, listeners always want to know, "What's your secret to success?" They think, *If you give me the secret button to push, I'll push it, and I'll be just like you.*

Spoiler alert: there is no secret sauce to building a successful business, team, ministry, or family. There is no single organizational or leadership technique that ensures profitability, scalability, growth, impact, or health in every part of our life and leadership.

From a lifestyle perspective, there is, however, one thing that can help you walk the daily road of God-pleasing leadership: *faithfulness*. A commitment to do the daily hard work and entrust the results to God.

The challenge is that this daily work is *hard*. It is painful, it is lonely, and it can be heartbreaking. It requires mega amounts of perseverance, and it requires a buffalo mentality to not run from the hard things but face them head-on.

Oswald Chambers, reflecting on Joshua 24:15 in his famous *My Utmost for His Highest*, says that we must "will to be faithful."[19] He encourages us to openly declare to God, "I will be faithful."

Have you made that commitment to the Lord? If not, will you?

The next section of this book is designed to help unpack the commitments we need to make before the Lord to lead and love in the daily hard work of faithfulness.

At the end of each chapter, there will be a handful of summarized "Faithful Leader Commitments" provided. My recommendation is to take the commitments that challenge you the most, write them on some index cards, and place them at strategic locations throughout your daily routine. My wife and I have used our bathroom mirror, kitchen sink, car dashboard, and desk for similar reminders.

THE LIFESTYLE OF A FAITHFUL LEADER

But here's a truth we don't always think about: God's glorious agenda for our ambition, like his glorious gospel, begins not with what we achieve but with who we are.[20]

DAVE HARVEY

5

SURRENDER

The goal of faithfulness is not that we will do work for God, but that He will be free to do His work through us.

OSWALD CHAMBERS

VINCE VITALE HAS a powerful short vlog entitled "Conversation As a Spiritual Discipline." In the video, Vitale shares how conversation can be used to fuel deeper, Christ-centered discussion. He shares a simple tip in the video:

> Usually, what is really going on in someone's heart is only two or three questions below the surface.[21]

The questions we ask *in response* to answers given to our previous questions are called connected questions. When we ask connected questions, we can quickly get past the surface and closer to someone's heart.

I decided to try this with a client one day over the phone.

"How's the business been?"

Question number one.

"How has that issue you just shared challenged you as a leader?"
Connected question number one.

It only took a single connected question, and we were off to the races: management difficulties, culture issues, fear, and uncertainty—it was all on the table. He asked if we could get lunch to continue the conversation, and, within a few days, we were together eating tacos.

Over lunch, we spoke about our religious backgrounds. He shared that he was Jewish. His parents had raised him with some Jewish practices, but he felt that he was, at this point, only culturally Jewish. Transparently, he said to me, "I've been raised around all these Judaic practices, but I've always felt like there was something more."

I said to him softly with excitement, "Let me introduce you to Him," and for the rest of the conversation, we spoke about Jesus, the gospel, and stories I had heard of Jews surrendering their lives to this Jewish, promised Messiah.

"Brandon, that's a really powerful word: *surrender*," he commented. "Surrendering is hard."

I agree with my friend. Surrendering is hard.

Surrendering is an act of submission and a willing forfeiture of control. It is the cessation of resistance and a handing over of something of value: our lives, our businesses, our will, our family, our children, our ministry, and even our success.

The life of a faithful leader is characterized by surrender. Regardless of the circumstances or the outcome, whether positive or negative, the faithful leader willingly yields to God's plan for his or her life and leadership, declaring, "My life and all I have is Yours. Use me however You want."

SUFFERING, PAIN, AND FAILURE

In a book entitled *Sex, Romance, and the Glory of God*, I read the story of Benjamin B. Warfield, a renowned theologian.[22] After his marriage to Annie Pierce

Kinkead at the age of 25, the couple decided to take a honeymoon in Leipzig, Germany, where he was studying.

On a walking trip through the mountains, a fierce thunderstorm overtook them and Annie was struck by lightning. The impact on Mrs. Warfield was so devastating that she never completely regained her health after the traumatic incident, and she remained largely incapacitated for the rest of her life due to the toll it took on her nervous system. "Because of her extraordinary needs, Warfield seldom left his home for more than two hours at a time during all those thirty-nine years of marriage."[23]

By all earthly definitions, this marriage was destined for failure. This couple's young, excited, newlywed marriage would now become a lifetime of spoon-fed dinners and wheelchair walks. They would never be able to experience the joy of God-pleasing sexual intimacy in their marriage.

I often ask myself, *Would I be faithful in a similar circumstance?*

Measuring our faithfulness in an unknown scenario is impossible, but it does make me stop and think about areas of my life that need growth.

Benjamin Warfield didn't get the "outcome" he wanted for his marriage (neither did his bride), but he surrendered to God's plan. He chose to glorify God in their brokenness, pain, and unmet expectations.

Similarly, by all earthly definitions, Jesus' death on the cross was an absolute failure.

The man who proclaimed that those who placed their faith in Him would never experience death was now Himself lifeless on a cross. Even as Jesus endured the agony of the cross, people scornfully taunted Him, saying, "Ha! Aren't you the so-called Chosen One?" From a purely human standpoint, Jesus' death was a failure, an unjust act of violence against a kind and compassionate teacher.

However, what appeared to be a failure to mankind was, in fact, God's triumph. It was God's divine plan to utilize this horrific event to ensure the ultimate redemption of His people.

Joseph's story, captured in Genesis 37 and 39–50, is another story filled with many perceived "defeats." Joseph was sold by his brothers into slavery, then falsely accused of adultery by his master's wife, and spent years in prison. After being released from prison and rising to second in command of all Egypt, he was reunited with his brothers and told them about all the things that had been done to him because of their actions against him, saying, "You meant evil against me, but God meant it for good" (Genesis 50:20).

According to God's operational model, evil and failure serve a greater purpose for good.

One of the guys who used to disciple me would say, "Immature Christians ask, 'Why!? Why are You doing this to me, God!?' But mature Christians ask, 'What? What are You trying to teach me in the middle of this, Lord?'"

This is what faithful leaders are constantly on the lookout for.

Our lives are filled with unmet expectations, unforeseen tragedies, and undesirable outcomes. From our point of view, those often look like great failures. But, as we've already seen, God is sovereign over all our experiences. It is the Lord who plots out our path, using each moment of pain, suffering, and failed outcomes to shape us.

Proverbs 16:9 says, "The heart of man plans his way, but the LORD establishes his steps."

If we had the eyes of the Lord and could see His grand narrative, we'd see a red thread being knit through each mountaintop and valley in our lives that ultimately leads to our mature faithfulness and obedience to Christ.

I was able to visit theologian R. C. Sproul's church only once before his passing, but I remember vividly this simple, pivotal question he asked regarding God's sovereign control over our lives: "Would you have it any other way?"

At the end of the day, would you really want your life ordered by anyone or anything other than the faithful, all-knowing, always-loving, wise, and generous Creator? Surrender your plans and look for those teaching moments from the Lord.

YOUR PAIN IS FOR OTHER PEOPLE

The first couple years of my marriage were not healthy. I thought it was awesome, but my wife knew the truth: we were broken. We loved each other and Jesus, but we hadn't seen great examples of two sinful people coming together to say day after day, "I do."

Knowing we needed to grow, we sought out discipleship opportunities through our church. The pastor of the church and his wife began to meet with us each week for some pretty in-your-face counseling.

One night, over a discussion at the dinner table, our pastor opened up the Bible and read 2 Corinthians 1:3–4:

> Blessed be the God and Father of our Lord Jesus Christ, the Father of mercies and God of all comfort, who comforts us in all our affliction, so that we may be able to comfort those who are in any affliction, with the comfort with which we ourselves are comforted by God.

Our pastor then told us, "Everything that you are being brought through right now is for a purpose. One day, you'll sit across the table from another couple struggling with some of the exact same things you are, and you'll be able to look them in the eyes and tell them, 'We've been where you are. Here is what God taught us.'" That moment has come true so many times.

Part of our surrendering to God means accepting that He will use pain and suffering to help us grow, so we can help others grow in the future. What journeys have you been on that you can use to encourage another person? What levels of surrender to God's plan did you have to get to as you grew? What comfort did you receive that you can pay forward? Faithful leader, look for opportunities to share those stories with the people around you.

WEAKNESS AND REST

In my early 30s, I began to have some strange health scares show up in my life: sharp pains in my head, unusual tiredness, mental fogginess, and vertigo, among other things. I saw a physical therapist, who pointed me to a specialized vertigo therapist, who pointed me to an allergist, who told me that he would not perform any more tests on me until I completed a brain MRI. What the MRI result would be was clear in my mind: *I 100% have a brain tumor.*

Though I enjoy diving in caverns underground, the thought of being put into a small MRI tube freaked me out. After two months of mentally convincing myself to participate in this medical nightmare, a brand new MRI facility opened in my hometown, Gainesville, Florida, with the largest scanner in the city, and I decided to go.

The results came back the morning after my visit: "Mr. West's brain is completely unremarkable." I was offended but encouraged. Maybe get some more bedside manner training?

I went on vacation for two weeks, and when I came back, the symptoms were gone.

Six months later, I arrived at church for an Easter rehearsal, and my heart started to beat strangely. Every 30 seconds or so, it felt like my heart skipped a beat and would take my breath away. Having to visit a cardiologist and wear a heart monitor in my early 30s didn't feel right. This isn't how I had pictured my youthful years.

After an EKG and a stress test (basically the worst running exercise of my entire life), the results came back a week later: "Mr. West's heart is completely unremarkable." After being serenaded by doctors with the harmonious chorus of "unremarkable" for both my brain and heart, I was going to need emotion-focused therapy, but at least my organs were healthy.

I was confused. Where were my symptoms coming from? What the heck was going on?

I resisted the inevitable conclusion: *stress*.

I used to think stress was a lie. I believed it was a word that weak people used to justify their self-care. "I'm stressed, so I'm going to the spa for the day" was a good way for people to shut down haters who questioned how they could spend money and time on massages or fishing trips.

My body was telling me a different story. I had to admit that stress is a formidable opponent—and that it had been winning.

For years, because I trivialized the ill effects of stress, I also trivialized its antidote. People in my sphere of influence would talk about the need for rest and retreat in leadership. But not me: I didn't require such personal indulgences. I would tell myself, *I'm a high-capacity leader. I don't need to waste time on recharging.*

Eventually, my body crashing forced me to change my tune. That's when I started noticing stress besieging other high-capacity leaders who refused to rest and retreat.

At one of my monthly C12 meetings, fellow business leaders and I were going around the table discussing our personal life and leadership highs and lows for the past 30 days. The 10 areas we asked each other about included our walk with God, nutrition and fitness, biblical community, and rest and retreat.

One of the members in the forum shared that his low was in rest and retreat. In love, I pointed out that it had been months since he reported anything other than *low* in that area of his life. I dug in a little, "Why do you not think rest and retreat is important in your life?"

"I honestly don't know," he replied.

Later in the meeting, he exclaimed, "I've got it! I know why I don't think rest and retreat are important!" He had this look of troubled wonder on his face as he shared, "I have a fear of failure. If I'm not doing something, I feel like a failure."

He didn't want to rest because rest felt like failure.

Doesn't our incessant striving originate from this very place? Isn't this the reason why we struggle to utter the word *no*?

We don't want to rest because we feel like we should always be doing something and producing something. It is the epitome of the outcome-based mindset.

In several seasons of my life, I have given myself so violently to the things I felt "called to" that I became empty emotionally, physically, and spiritually.

I can think of multiple date nights with my wife or sons when I felt so emotionally depleted that they probably would have preferred dining with a crash test dummy instead of me. I would appear almost catatonic as they attempted to engage me in conversation. On one date night with my 14-year-old son, just as we were exiting a grocery store, I handed him my phone and said, "Be prepared to dial 911." My body had started to shut down: my vision blurred, strong vertigo set in, my head went flush, and my heart was racing. Though I didn't end up in the hospital that night, it clearly wasn't the fun night I had planned with my son.

The outcome-based mindset will kill us. But, when we abandon that mindset, we find a universe of new freedoms.

> The world may celebrate a hustle culture where "10x at any cost" is the badge of honor, but as sons and daughters of God, we're invited to life in a different Kingdom, where the economy of success is anchored in the gospel.[24]

Faithful leaders rest well because they define success differently than the world does.

Faithful leaders rest well because they know their ultimate outcomes are not in their own hands, and they can trust them to a faithful God.

Faithful leaders rest well because God does.

Over and over, I have had to surrender to the limitations of my humanity, my production capacity, and the needs of my mind and body. Through that process, I have started to look at self-care very differently. "If I want to care for other people, then I better start caring for myself, or I won't be able to care for them." I even worked this into our leadership development program at PHOS in a lecture titled "Unselfish Self-Care | How to Invest in You for Others."

By integrating new rhythms of daily, weekly, and twice-a-month retreats into my schedule, I have found new levels of creativity, innovation, and self-learning. By prioritizing rest, I have ensured that I have enough left in me to do the daily hard work of faithfulness at work and at home.

Resting and retreating don't make you a failure, but failing to rest may lead to your physical, emotional, and spiritual failure. If Jesus spent time resting and retreating, what makes you think you don't need what He made time for in His own life?

Maybe a lack of rest and retreat in your life is evidence you're holding on to an outcome-based mindset. Your healthy faithfulness in the future requires a surrender to your fragility and an investment into regular cadences of rest and retreat.

> Born to work, even to excess.
> Born-again to trust, even to rest.
> Hustling and trusting, which is best?
> Managing the tension with the gospel of rest.[25]

CHASING THINGS I COULD GIVE UP

As PHOS was growing, we had an opportunity to buy an incredible piece of property to build on. The property was near my house (cutting my driving time by more than half), was brand new, and was being designed by a smart, local architect. I wanted this property *bad.*

Every morning, as I passed it on my drive into the office, I would pray over the property with great expectation. Eventually, I reached out to a local real estate friend and had him prepare a letter of intent that I signed and returned to begin the planning process.

In due diligence, I began to crunch the numbers for the increased mortgage expenses, and, as I did so, God began to reveal a different plan that was going to crush this dream.

As I discussed the opportunity with Alexis, our director of operations, we began to see more pressing needs at PHOS. How could we invest all this money into a building for PHOS when we were not yet offering our team members any significant paid benefits? We had already seen at least one person leave the company because we had yet to implement a benefits program. Were we really willing to invest thousands of extra dollars each month into this space when we already had a pretty cool one?

My first answer was, "Uhhh, YES! This is an investment!" But that wasn't God's plan.

As I drove to work each morning and passed the plot of land, it became clear to me that I had a choice: invest in a building or invest in our people.

It took me longer than it ought to have, but I surrendered to this truth: people have a better return on investment than a building.

Faithfulness in my leadership role required the death of my dreams.

It doesn't always feel good to make the hard decision. That is where the question "What do you have peace about?" begins to fail us.

Not every dream we have is a dream God wants us to pursue.

The faithful leader says, "Here are my dreams and goals, Lord; do what you want with them." We find contentment in following God's plans, even when they contradict our own.

I saw a post on Facebook recently in which someone was quoting Benjamin Mays, who said, "The tragedy of life doesn't lie in not reaching your goals. The tragedy lies in having no goals to reach."

While I agree that there is a level of regret about not living intentionally, I disagree that the tragedy of life is having no goals. The tragedy of life is living your whole life chasing goals and dreams that don't matter. The tragedy lies in being ambitiously committed to a dream that should have been surrendered in pursuit of something greater and better.

What are those dreams in your life? What dreams are you pursuing that are costing you your profits, your team, your marriage, your children, your ministry, and maybe even yourself?

In their song "Lead Me," Sanctus Real asks for God to lead them so they are able to lead their wives and children well. They cry out to God to give them the strength to be what they are called to be and to give their family the best of themselves because they "Don't want to leave them hungry for love / Chasing things that I could give up."[26]

You will never regret the dreams you give up to faithfully lead and love those entrusted to you. Don't leave your family, your team, your church, or your community hungry for love while you're chasing things you could give up. Surrender those things to the Lord.

What is the dream worth pursuing and giving ourselves to? Jeremy Riddle, in his book on worship, writes,

> So many are chasing the wrong dream and the empty thing. Forgive me an Ecclesiastical moment while I cry out, "Vanity of vanities. All is vanity!" My friends, the dream is nothing . . . worse than nothing . . . without Him. Better is one day in His presence than a lifetime of fulfilled dreams without Him. HE . . . is the dream. Faithfulness to Jesus is the dream! The only dream worth living for![27]

Maybe something needs to change in your life. Maybe your dreams are off. Maybe you've been chasing the wrong thing. You can start that change today, but it may mean surrendering your dreams that don't match God's dreams for you. Be faithful and don't look back.

LEARNING TO DREAM NEW DREAMS

When I was nine years old, my dad helped me construct my first-ever Dream Book. His Dream Book framework included categorized photographs, magazine cutouts, and notebook pages that documented dreams I had for my life. It outlined things I wanted to own, places I wanted to visit, jobs I wanted to have, and salaries I wanted to hit. It was a fun activity and a strong shared memory with my father.

Over the years, I've made updates to this Dream Book, helping me to live a fairly vision-driven life.

Unfortunately, by the time I was 34, I had, for the most part, completed most of the dreams I actually cared about. I realized this most acutely when I watched a video about Renee Lockey called "Work Like a Doctor, Live Like a Nurse." Renee is a career obstetrician with a big salary.

The first time I watched this video, I was so struck when Renee said that, by the time she was 37, she "had accomplished everything [she] had set out to accomplish." At that moment, I realized where some of the emptiness I was feeling inside was coming from. I had completed my dreams. What was left? It had to be more than just a bigger house, a better car, more vacations, and a larger retirement account.

Renee's commitment to working like a doctor and living like a nurse led her to create a budget for the first time in a long time, and she started living off a quarter of her salary. She used the other 75% to serve the needs of others.

I started doing more research and listening to the stories of other faithful, generous business owners who were doing wildly radical things to serve the needs of others. I learned about Simon Lee's commitment since day one of his business, Buy on Purpose, to give away 50% of their profit. I learned about Alan Barnhart's vision for Barnhart Crane & Rigging to move from one million dollars a year in corporate giving to one million dollars a *month* in corporate giving. They now exceed that goal every year.

As I heard these stories, I was learning to surrender to an entirely new definition of financial success and future planning. I was learning to ask new questions and dream new dreams.

If everything I have is God's, what does He want me to do with it?

What if my next dreams in life weren't about me but dreams that I could dream for other people?

As I unpacked these new questions and convictions, I learned new levels of surrender in others-centered living. We hear things like "people over profit," but how have those forms of thinking actually affected our profit and loss statements? How have they shaped our financial management and corporate giving strategies?

If you built out your Dream Book, would there be a section for dreams you have for serving others? Which section would be the most packed with dreams? Which section would get you the most excited?

Maybe for you, the challenge isn't to give up a dream that isn't worth chasing; maybe it's learning to chase a dream you've never considered. Our call to faithful leadership is going to challenge the dreams we have and force us to redefine success away from accomplishing things for ourselves and instead toward meeting the needs of others.

PURPOSE, NOT POTENTIAL

One of the biggest cultural evils of our day is the phrase "wasted potential." It's a label we apply to underperforming children and adults: "They are wasting their potential."

The law of potential says, "If I can do it, I should do it. If I have the potential to do it, I must, because the last thing I want at the end of my life is to leave potential sitting on the table."

By this definition, Jesus did not fulfill His potential.

During His time on earth, how many more hurting people could Jesus have healed? How many more lost people could He have reached? How many wicked and godless rulers could He have overthrown to rescue His people from adversity and affliction?

He had the potential to do so. But He did not. Why? Because that wasn't His purpose.

Jesus did not fulfill His potential, but He did completely fulfill His purpose. That was enough for Him. Jesus' pace allowed Him personal quiet times with the Father, one-on-one discipleship moments with His closest friends, and regular, fruitful, public times of ministry.

You could do a billion things with your life and your gifts. Your potential is nearly limitless.

But what if you capped your investment in your potential to ensure that you faithfully executed the duties of your calling?

Faithful leaders are willing to surrender potential to protect their pace.

In pursuit of your purpose, you will not be able to fulfill your potential. If you focus your time on the things you are *called* to, you will not have time for everything you *could* do.

I'm not talking about disregarding potential or choosing to neglect potential—that is not faithful leadership. I'm talking about surrendering your potential when and where your calling demands it.

Let's consider two scenarios:

1. You're a wife, you have huge career goals, and you got pregnant. You've chosen to stay at home with your children, and now you may

be thinking, *I'm wasting my potential in the marketplace by being at home all day with my children.*

No! This is precisely where God is calling you to invest yourself. Be faithful.

2. You're managing a team, you have developed a high-performing group, and your widowed mom falls, breaks her hip, and has no one to care for her. Now you're traveling back and forth for hours each week and may be thinking, *I'm wasting my potential with my team by traveling and providing medical care for my mom.*

   No! This is exactly where God is calling you to give yourself away. Be faithful.

I've heard both of these stories, and they are heartbreaking.

Faithful leaders aren't plagued by the question, "Why didn't you do more?" because they are content with knowing they did what they were supposed to.

Success, then, is not about doing everything you are capable of but about doing the things you've been called to do. Faithful leaders content themselves with surrendered potential because they find their success not in their accomplishments but in their pursuit of faithfulness.

FOCUS IS A TOOL FOR FAITHFULNESS

I am a huge fan of escape games. If you've never done one, picture being locked in a themed room for 60 minutes and using only the available clues to escape. (I know it sounds like the plot of a low-budget thriller. You should try it anyway.) Problem solving, team building, and adventure. It's a blast.

After completing more than 30 rooms, I had an idea for starting my own. I envisioned a Narnia-themed room, where you stepped through a wardrobe into a fantastical space, and a *Jurassic Park*-inspired room. Every team that escaped was going to help fund rescue missions for children escaping trafficking overseas. It was a beautiful, creative idea.

I was excited to launch a second business with it.

During a review with one of my financial advisors in Orlando, I shared the vision I had for starting this second business. Tony is a New York-born, Floridian mobster (not really, but it feels that way when he talks), who always shoots me straight.

When I pitched the idea to Tony, his reaction was historic: "What!? Shut your mouth, and go milk your cash cow!" In other words, go focus on the company you already have; you don't need a second one.

Right or wrong, that advice has helped to keep me singularly focused on PHOS. While I could have started that business, not starting it has helped me remain faithful in my role at the business God had already given me to steward.

Maybe you are called to be a serial entrepreneur or open a bunch more locations for your business, but maybe that's not what's best for your spouse, your children, or your ministry. Maybe that's not even what's best for you. What you can know for sure is that God desires you to be faithful and committed to excellence.

If you do feel called to invest yourself in a plurality of professional, social, and communal activities, at least answer this question: What are you valuing that is compelling your desire for more?

If the answer is God-centered and Kingdom-oriented, move forward confidently in faithfulness. If it's not, maybe this is a moment to surrender your potential and be faithful where you are called.

Maybe you've already overextended yourself and invested in things you shouldn't have, and you're wondering, *How can I ever get out of this?* I know this sounds so much easier than it actually is, but you need to take the loss. It's difficult, it's embarrassing, and it can be crazy costly, but it's worth it for the people you love.

I was recently reading in 2 Chronicles about a man who did what was right in the eyes of the Lord . . . sometimes. The story explains that as he was about to go out into battle, he was counseled not to bring one of the tribes with him because they weren't on God's side. I so resonate with his response: "But what about all the money I've already paid them to fight with us!?" But the prophet tells him, "The LORD is able to give you much more than this" (2 Chronicles 25:9).

What excuses are you using that are keeping you from surrendering and being faithful to do what you know you should?

Maybe you could grow your business by 50–500% next year, but maybe it's not worth it. Maybe doing so will force you and your team to sacrifice faithful leadership in other areas of your lives. **Intentionally inhibited growth may be your greatest tool to help you maintain faithful leadership over yourself, your team, and your family.**

If you have the potential for more, but that's not God's plan, who are you to say to the Potter, why have you made me this way (Isaiah 45:9)?

More is not always best. Being faithful is best, and that may require surrendering your potential.

WILLINGLY OUTSHONE

One of the most refreshing books on marriage that I have read has been Gary Thomas' book *Cherish*. Though we commit at a wedding ceremony to "love and cherish" one another, Thomas argues that, while people talk a lot about *love*, we haven't sufficiently covered *cherish*.[28]

In one of the chapters, he lays out a powerful analogy about what cherishing our spouse looks like: a ballet. I know almost nothing about ballet, but I can picture the scene clearly.

Ballerinas are capable of incredible physical feats, but when a cavalier (a male dancing partner) assists them on stage, they are able to do more. With their partners' help, the dancers are able to jump higher, spin faster, and perform more complex ballet moves. When the routine ends, the helper, dressed in all black, steps back toward the black curtain, fading out of the audience's view, and the ballerina steps forward on the stage, into the spotlight, to receive their applause.[29] The cavalier thus *cherishes* the ballerina: he enables, assists, and sacrifices to promote her flourishing.

Faithful leadership is about using our gifts, strengths, and influence to help other people. When the spotlight comes on, faithful leaders love reflecting it back on others. They find their success in the success of others, even if that means they take the back seat during the applause.

Puritan author Thomas Watson wrote, "A humble man is willing to have his name and [gifts] eclipsed, so God's glory may be more increased; he is content to be outshined by others in gifts and esteem, so that the crown of Christ may shine the brighter."[30]

Faithful leaders recognize that increased prestige or a bigger platform can threaten their genuine, authentic, and others-centered leadership. They understand that the spotlight, at times, can actually become a stumbling block to their faithful leadership. Their greatest joys lie in giving away their influence and leadership to other people: lifting up, empowering, and propelling the people around them to greater heights. They surrender the spotlight to see Christ and others shine.

EXCITED TO SURRENDER

If we are going to walk with Jesus faithfully, we are going to have to surrender, then resurrender, over and over.

Corrie ten Boom said it this way: "Hold everything in your hands loosely; otherwise, it hurts when God pries your fingers open."[31] We need to hold tightly to God and loosely to everything else.

To what are you holding on too tightly? Where do you need to surrender results to the Lord? What are you pursuing so hard that you are causing people in your life to suffer because you think you are responsible for the results?

Faithful leaders surrender regularly to God's plans for their results, God's plans for their suffering, God's plans for their rest, God's plans for their gifts and potential, and God's plans for their shared leadership. Faithful leaders surrender to second position in all aspects of their lives. They know that God is in control, so they content themselves with His leading, joyfully stepping aside to watch Him at work.

I admire some of the people in my C12 forum who seem to have really big faith in God. When something unexpected comes up, a plan falls through, or a big loss happens in their business, instead of their first reaction being frustration or fear, it's excitement. They are genuinely excited to see where the Lord is going to lead. "I thought it was this thing, but since I now know it's not, I can't wait to see what God is going to do!"

I'm not like them yet, but I want this level of surrender in my life.

When we surrender, we position ourselves, our businesses, and our families to walk faithfully with God into every season of our lives.

> I am no longer my own but yours.
> Put me to what you will,
> rank me with whom you will;
> put me to doing,
> put me to suffering;
> let me be employed for you,
> or laid aside for you,
> exalted for you,
> or brought low for you;
> let me be full,
> let me be empty,
> let me have all things,
> let me have nothing:
> I freely and wholeheartedly yield all things
> to your pleasure and disposal.
> And now, glorious and blessed God,
> Father, Son and Holy Spirit,
> you are mine and I am yours. So be it.[32]

FAITHFUL LEADER COMMITMENTS

01 I will surrender to God's plan in times of suffering, seeking to learn the lessons He is teaching me and finding ways to share those lessons with others.

02 I will surrender to God's plan for rest and retreat, embracing my weaknesses as reminders of my need for God.

03 I will surrender my dreams to the Lord, challenging myself to seek God for dreams that He might have me dream for other people.

04 I will surrender my potential to the Lord, focusing instead on fulfilling His purpose in and through me.

05 I will surrender my need for control and embrace God's sovereignty, trusting His ultimate purpose in every situation.

06 I will surrender my own ambitions and seek God's direction, aligning my leadership goals with His Kingdom agenda.

6

BECOMING

What you get by achieving your goals is not as important as what you become by achieving your goals.

ZIG ZIGLAR

OW DO YOU define a successful day?

If you're like most people, it's when you have a giant checklist of to-dos at the beginning of the day, then at the end of the day you do not. The more you check off, the more successful your day has been!

What if tomorrow you actually completed all your checklists? I'm talking about *every* checklist: your "Big Three," the rest of your daily to-dos, your honey-do list, and your "wouldn't it be great" list. All of them, done. What a great day, right!?? You'd be sending selfies to *Success* magazine and expecting to see your face on the next issue's cover.

But what if, in the process of checking all those things off, you were a jerk all day long? What if you were frustrated and angry with people who got in your way as you worked through your lists? What if you spoke rudely to your spouse when he or she questioned your priorities? What if you were impatient with your children when they interrupted your work? What if you neglected team members or clients you knew needed your leadership and feedback? Would it still have been a successful day?

Faithful leaders who have untethered themselves from the trap of outcome-based thinking see their success in ways much more meaningful than completed to-dos and finished projects. They don't just ask themselves questions about progress: *How close am I to getting the things that I want?* They ask themselves more probing questions about their character. They labor over this crucial question:

Who am I becoming in pursuit of what I want?

Answer that honestly for yourself right now.

Who are you becoming in pursuit of the things you want? What kind of person are your dreams turning you into? Have you made your boss or your dad proud of your accomplishments, but your spouse can't stand you? Is your financial planner pleased with your books, but your team and your children despise you?

Be honest with yourself: who have you become over the past 2 to 10 years?

You can be successful in every way that our culture applauds and still be a failure.

Your character, the health of your soul, and who you are becoming are at the heart of God's will for your life and leadership. These are at the heart of success, as God measures it. To support this agenda, God will bring into our lives, or take from our lives, whatever it is that will invite us to become more like Him.

This understanding of God's sovereignty in our circumstances, and of His priority in shaping our character, gives us hope. As Paul wrote,

> And I am sure of this, that he who began a good work in you will bring it to completion at the day of Jesus Christ. (Philippians 1:6)

In other words, we know that God brings every season into our lives, the painful ones and the peaceful ones, to guide us in our becoming who He wants us to be.

SEMPER REFORMANDA

Though our journey toward becoming is about becoming more like God, God is not on a similar journey. He is the same yesterday, today, and forever. God does not become something better. He does not need to. We do.

For God to be faithful, He cannot change.

For us to be faithful, we must change.

Change is hard, but it's always easier if we accept it willingly. That means accepting that God wants to change us through the work He has given us.

This makes sense, given what we know of faithfulness: **Faithfulness is daily hard work entrusted to God**.

Faithful leaders are committed to growing and changing and learning because they understand, *I am not yet all God has called me to be, but I'll go after it faithfully.*

If we have willingly embarked on a journey of becoming, then we have already confessed that we are not all that either God or we desire us to be. If we know that, then why are we still so resistant to change?

Theologian and author Kevin DeYoung writes, "If no one has ever heard you change your mind about something, then you are either a god or you have mistaken yourself for one."[33]

For years I had an unspoken assumption that a faithful leader doesn't change. *A faithful leader sets a plan and sees it through to the end*, I thought. *They create a culture and ensure it does not evolve. That's their job.*

Then the world went through a global crisis, and all plans had to change. And with adjusted plans came a massive workforce shift, in which I realized flexibility is vital—not only to survival but also to a healthy company culture.

John Spence, a global author and speaker from my home city, shared in a TEDx talk about the three competencies of the leader of the future. The first two are familiar: a leader's intelligence quotient (IQ; "I'm good at what I do") and their emotional quotient (EQ; "I can understand the people I work with"). The third, Spence argues, is possibly the most important competency of the future: a leader's agility or adaptability quotient (AQ; "I am able to navigate change").[34]

Our ability to not only manage change but actually lead corporate evolution is one of the most important leadership competencies of future leaders.

Faithful leadership isn't about sticking to your plans when you should abandon them. It's about sticking to your God-given purpose even when your plans fail. This entails being willing to question your plans and to be questioned in pursuit of them, then course correct where necessary.

I remember times in my organization when I made grand, sweeping statements about what PHOS would forever do and be committed to. "We'll never have remote work team members." Now we do. "We'll always be a five-day-a-week-in-the-office company." Now we aren't (we have a hybrid work model).

Craig Groeschel, pastor of Life.Church, says bold declarations like these can help to inspire teams—but he also says when things change, leaders must be willing to "unmake a promise."[35] That's different, Groeschel says, than breaking a promise. Unmaking a promise is about owning your prior commitments, embracing organizational learning, and aligning your future corporate strategy more closely to your present reality—one that may have shifted dramatically. Sometimes those early declarations we make can wind up limiting our leadership impact if we become unwilling to unmake our promises.

Sadly, it's easy to confuse our commitments. We must regularly (even daily!) ask ourselves whether we are more committed to our plans or to God's purpose for us, to our outcomes or to faithfulness, to our imaginary self-portrait or to the reflection of Jesus' character in our lives.

In other words, we must always be reforming our plans to ensure they conform with God's purpose. Doing so, however, may radically alter the trajectory of our life and leadership. (That's a good thing.)

I remember when we received our first negative review online from a team member who had quit. I was heartbroken, and it took me a while to process the feedback before I could respond. At the counsel of my peers, I decided to leverage the moment for team learning. During a company-wide team meeting, we put the review up on the screen and asked what was true about it. What can we learn? Then we asked how we wanted to respond, and, together as a team, we crafted the response and posted it online. It was a painful but powerful time of uniting the team. Below is our combined response.

> A review like this truly breaks our hearts. We're thankful that this is unusually inconsistent with others' feedback, but it nonetheless causes us to pause and consider. In an effort to pursue the highest levels of transparency and accountability, we reviewed all these points with our advisors and gathered the entire team to hear their hearts on these matters. Here is what your team wanted to share with you:
>
> "Whoever you are, we miss you! Our hearts are heavy knowing that you didn't feel loved by the team. We take great joy in being with one another, and you were a part of that PHamily."
>
> "We truly want to be 'a place that team members never want to leave' (our mission). The past year, we've made some huge changes to our compensation packages, benefits offerings, and processes that have helped with this, and we've got lots more coming."
>
> [From the CEO]
> Being a part of the team at PHOS, you would have likely heard me say this at some point: "semper reformanda." During the Reformation, this phrase stood as a banner over the church to say, "We are always reforming." We have flown that flag over PHOS since the day we started, primarily because we have needed to. We are constantly in need of more growth and more grace.

It's hard to share open and honest feedback, so I commend you for doing so. I only wish you would have shared it sooner so we could have grown together. Despite these harsh words, we still love you, and I would warmly welcome the opportunity to meet, eat some tacos, and reconcile with one another.

The faithful leader is always reforming, always changing, always becoming.

The outcome-based mindset says we need to achieve our results at all costs, or we have failed. The faithfulness mindset says we ought to be willing to change anything necessary to serve the people we are leading best. A faithful leader is willing to ask *What's most important right now?* and course correct if current plans do not align.

To lead faithfully, we need to be willing to take a step back and take a pulse to see where we and our teams are. Then we need to be willing to adapt ourselves to that reality.

IN THE WAITING

I am naturally impatient. One personal assessment I took revealed that 98% of the world is more patient than I am. It's something I've struggled with for a long time and regularly have to work through. I don't like to wait.

Yet so much of my life has been filled with waiting.

I graduated from the University of Florida with an undergraduate degree in classical studies. At the time, my vocational trajectory was pastoral ministry, and I believed that classical studies was the best degree I could get in college to prepare myself for seminary.

One Sunday, at the beginning of my fourth year of college, I was connecting with a visiting pastor after church. Though it was the first time he and I had met, I shared my dreams of attending seminary and pursuing pastoral ministry. His advice was overly direct: "You are 21!? If you want to go into pastoral ministry, go get some life experience and get a job!" (Pro life tip: it's probably best not to be this direct until you've built some street cred with the person you're advising.)

Though I wasn't happy to hear that advice at the time, God used that conversation to redirect my heart and passions.

When I finished my degree at UF, I got a position teaching at a local Christ-centered classical school. I taught Greek and Latin language to middle school and high school students for four years until God led me to start PHOS.

Six years into PHOS (and a decade after the abrasive pastoral conversation), I was frustrated with my calling and my work. I felt called to be a pastor, but after 15 years in ministry at my church—leading worship thousands of times, facilitating hundreds of small groups, and providing hours of counseling for individuals and couples through every issue you can imagine—I still didn't have the title of "pastor."

One morning, while driving to the office, I was praying (or, more accurately, venting my frustrations), asking, "Why are you blessing PHOS so much, God!? You know the heart I have for pastoral ministry. You know the love I have for the local church. Why have you not allowed me to pursue that calling?"

It was probably one of the clearest times I have felt like I heard from the Lord. In my heart I heard Him say, "I *have* called you to be a pastor. I have called you to be a pastor of business leaders."

What clarity waiting can bring to the faithful leader! This was a breakthrough moment for me. It made me realize that the story being written that decade of my life involved both business and ministry, not just business alone.

In the middle of my waiting, God was making me into—I was *becoming*—who He wanted me to be.

Fireproof, one of the first Christian movies I ever watched, features a song called "While I'm Waiting," by John Waller. Waller writes,

> While I'm waiting, I will serve You
> While I'm waiting, I will worship
> While I'm waiting, I will not faint
> I'll be running the race
> Even while I wait[36]

That's what the faithful leader is committed to: serving, loving, leading, and worshiping, even while waiting. Why? Because faithful leaders trust that God is shaping us in our waiting, and we are confident that who we are becoming is more important than what we accomplish.

I wanted the title of pastor, but God wanted the heart of a pastor. He wanted my willingness to faithfully pastor in the waiting without a title.

I once had the pleasure of interviewing John Walsh, an executive at the Walt Disney Company, on stage at a leadership conference. Walsh is an incredible guy with a huge heart who has an amazing story of going from homelessness to intern to CFO. When we got down from the stage, he came up to me, gave me a hug, and thanked me for the interview, then looked me in the eyes and said, "If we ever get to do this again, don't ever introduce me as the Chief Financial Officer of Walt Disney. I don't want people to respect me because of my title. Go read Robin Sharma's book *The Leader Who Had No Title*." Walsh didn't want to be called by his title, because that wasn't what made him a leader.

God doesn't care about titles either. He cares about who you're becoming.

If you wait for a title before you start doing what God has purposed you to do, you'll be waiting a *very* long time to become the person He wants you to become.

Will you be faithful to serve God in the waiting, trusting that who you are becoming is more important than what you accomplish?

IN GOD'S TIMING

Success is following God's plan in God's timing.

My usual way of doing things is diving headfirst into my to-do list without even consulting God. Then, I'll look back, realize I didn't seek God's guidance at all, and pray in retrospect, "Hey, God, can you bless this decision I already made?" Or, alternatively, I'll rush into a decision just to avoid thinking about it, praying about it, or seeking advice because I want it to be "already done."

I am not being faithful in either of those scenarios. Here's where I need to be:

> The LORD is good to those who wait for him, to the soul who seeks him. (Lamentations 3:25)

This is trying for those who struggle with patience, but God sometimes wants us to wait. Waiting is a part of His plan for us to become more like Jesus. Dave Harvey writes in his book *Rescuing Ambition*,

> Waiting is often God's reorientation program aimed at our definition of success. He lovingly empties our misguided preoccupation with accomplishment and fills it with ambitions to know him and be like him. God isn't beyond slowing our walk to remind us that only he is omnipotent, and we're not; only he is omnicompetent, and we're not; only he exists without a need for rest, and we don't.[37]

Who are you becoming in pursuit of what you want? How is God using your time of waiting to grow your perseverance and faithfulness? What part of your definition of success is God trying to rewrite through your waiting?

WAITING VS. STOPPING

After leading PHOS through the new building vs. benefits package decision, I was happy with the choice to build a benefits package. We found some creative options that allowed us to build a fully funded and generous plan, resulting in increased retention of our staff.

But, as our team grew, we eventually ran out of space in our facility, and the building problem was back on the table.

We looked at every option: leasing more space where we were at, leasing a different space, purchasing an already existing space, building a new office, or buying our current space. One by one, every option got scratched from the list. Leasing an additional unit in our current building was the best option, but the cost comparison with buying the building wasn't making financial sense to me.

All our attempts to buy the space we were in also began to fall flat. Our landlord agreed to entertain an offer from us to purchase the building, but after presenting the offer through our realtor, the landlord changed her mind and said she wouldn't sell. I decided to meet with her one-on-one to work my galvanizing magic and cast vision for our mission, showing how the building has supported our impact in the community in the past and explaining all the good it would do in the future.

The outcome? Blank stare. Nothing.

We met with her one more time with a bunch of market research on pricing comparables and a higher offer. Her counter was another 10% higher than our offer, and I just didn't feel comfortable with that financial stretch. She stood up from the table and told me, "Brandon, this is the only way I'm selling. You better consider my offer," and walked out.

I went home engulfed by a sense of defeat and broke down in tears. My options had dwindled to none.

I took a walk around my community the next morning, and I prayed out loud, "Turn this situation into a God story. Do something so that, when it's over, all I'll be able to say is, 'God did this.'"

I got back to my computer, and I started to look for new options. All of them were too big or too expensive, but I had renewed confidence in my heart that the Lord would provide.

Thirty-six hours later, I got a call from my realtor. "Your landlord is going to accept your offer." *Say whaaaa!??* That is definitely not how I thought this story would play out.

Between my prayer and this call, I didn't stop looking for options. I stopped to pray, but I didn't stop searching. I moved forward, trying to discern what God had planned to answer that prayer with. Even that next week, I was still reviewing additional properties in case my landlord's commitment fell through. I didn't know what God would do, but I trusted He would be faithful.

Waiting faithfully is a posture of the heart that rests on God's own faithfulness. Waiting might mean stopping and doing nothing, but, for me, being faithful in the waiting has often looked like a continued commitment to do the hard work, trusting that in and through the process God is working on my behalf and, at the same time, inside of me.

> In the morning sow your seed, and at evening withhold not your hand, for you do not know which will prosper, this or that, or whether both alike will be good. (Ecclesiastes 11:6)

JUST-IN-TIME GROWING

We've established that God works in the waiting room to make us into the people He wants us to be.

But if that's where God does His work, doesn't that mean we'll be in the waiting room most of our lives?

Yes, in one way or another, since God is perpetually preparing us for our next season. But when it's game time in some aspect of our lives, He always makes sure we have what we need to faithfully follow Him.

Corrie ten Boom first faced the reality of death at a young age when a baby died in a neighboring family. When Corrie's father returned home the evening she had found out, Corrie burst into tears and shouted at her father, "You can't die! You can't!" She describes what happened next in her book *The Hiding Place*.

> Father sat down on the edge of the narrow bed. "Corrie," he began gently, "when you and I go to Amsterdam—when do I give you your ticket?"

> I sniffed a few times, considering this.
>
> "Why, just before we get on the train."
>
> "Exactly. And our wise Father in heaven knows when we're going to need things, too. Don't run out ahead of Him, Corrie. When the time comes that some of us will have to die, you will look into your heart and find the strength you need—just in time."[38]

Jesus did this with His disciples as well. In John 16, Jesus tells His disciples they are going to be persecuted and killed—but also that He is sending them a Helper to provide comfort.

That's quite a bombshell to drop on a bunch of guys who left everything to follow Jesus. Shouldn't He have told them sooner?

In verse 4, Jesus says, "I did not say these things to you from the beginning, because I was with you." Jesus didn't teach some of these things to His disciples earlier in their journey together, because He didn't need to. He was right there with them. But when Jesus says this, He is preparing them for His imminent departure. And even then, He keeps them on a need-to-know, just-in-time basis. A few verses later, He adds, "I still have many things to say to you, but you cannot bear them now" (John 16:12).

The Lord has lessons He wants to teach you that He will deliberately delay in teaching you. Because I want to get to the point quickly on things, it's challenging for me to accept that God provides the right things only at the right moment. If you're like me, you're thinking, *Lord, I want to know this now*. But God says, "When you're ready. My timing is perfect."

Why would God delay teaching you something that would be valuable for you to know?

- The lesson wouldn't make sense to you now.
- You need to grow in your trust and dependence on Him first.
- He is protecting you.

When Jesus told the disciples He was leaving and that they would face intense persecution, sorrow filled their hearts (John 16:6). Imagine how the disciples might have lived discouraged and hopeless if Jesus had told them this truth years before.

There are things I've learned in my becoming that have been so hard to process and grow through. I can't imagine going through them a decade ago. Those lessons are almost too heavy for me to handle now. They could have ruined me years ago.

Sometimes you're just not ready for something. Have you ever read a book, then reread it a few years later and thought, *Wow, I got so much more from this book the second time!* I doubt the majority of those times are because you weren't smart enough the first time you read it. Perhaps you simply weren't ready to receive it.

God knows your readiness level. He knows what you need. He knows your capabilities, strengths, and weaknesses, and He is compassionate and understanding with you. He knows the precise time and circumstances that will best teach you what you need to learn. As Solomon poetically put it, "He has made everything beautiful in its time" (Ecclesiastes 3:11).

In what areas of your life are you trying to run out ahead of God and need to instead be faithful to trust His timing and His process for your becoming?

THE OPPOSITE OF FRAGILE

If you haven't figured it out yet, I should probably break it to you: becoming who God wants you to be isn't easy (although it's still easier than being someone God *doesn't* want you to be).

When you think of something that is fragile, what do you think of? Probably something that is delicate and easily broken, maybe a specific item that sat in grandma's glass hutch that you couldn't touch, next to the couch you couldn't sit on, near the rug you couldn't walk on.

A fragile *person* is someone you constantly feel like you're tiptoeing around. You have to avoid certain topics, or else they won't talk to you for a week, a month . . . a year. If you dare to say anything other than praise, they completely lose it.

My friend once asked me, "What's the opposite of fragile?"

I thought about things that are durable, things made from strong materials, and things that don't break easily under pressure.

There are, however, various things in life that go beyond merely not breaking. These things actually grow stronger under pressure, thrive when damaged, and become increasingly resilient through adversity. They possess an inherent ability not only to withstand challenges but actually to flourish and evolve through them.

Nassim Nicholas Taleb invented his own word to describe this. He says,

> Some things benefit from shocks; they thrive and grow when exposed to volatility, randomness, disorder, and stressors and love adventure, risk, and uncertainty. Yet, in spite of the ubiquity of the phenomenon, there is no word for the exact opposite of fragile. Let us call it antifragile. Antifragility is beyond resilience or robustness. The resilient resists shocks and stays the same; the antifragile gets better.[39]

Consider your muscles, which require their fibers to be torn apart through exercise before they can grow back together stronger. Or diamonds, which are formed out of coal by immense pressure. Or the sedimentary rock that makes up countless square miles of mountainous terrain across the whole globe—also formed by pressure. Or a chinese finger trap. Or a knot.[40] Pressure is transformative.

My pastor used to tell me, "You can't see what's inside the toothpaste container until you squeeze it. When *you* get squeezed, what comes out?"

Most of life is the vanilla, nonessential, "How you doing?" "Good" kind of stuff. It's really not until the toothpaste container gets squeezed that you realize who you are becoming on the inside.

Are you becoming more fragile or more antifragile? Do hard times strengthen your resolve or cause your card castle to come crumbling down?

During my struggles with heart dysrhythmia, I received a phone call from Mike Gilland, a close friend and mentor, who wanted to check in on me. In that conversation, he encouraged me with this verse:

> For the righteous will never be moved;
> He will be remembered forever.
> He is not afraid of bad news;
> His heart is firm, trusting in the LORD. (Psalm 112:6–7)

When the pressure is on, when the vice grip is tightening, when the lights are starting to go dim, what happens to your heart? Righteous people don't fear bad news. Their hearts hold firm.

Leaders are under such regular, extreme heat and severe pressure that—should they learn to be antifragile—the pure carbon they start with can form into beautiful, rare character diamonds through the metamorphic process of becoming.

FRUITFULNESS FROM FIRE

Serotiny is an ecological adaptation that causes a plant to drop its seeds after it experiences a certain environmental trigger. These serotinous seeds develop gradually over time, and, before they flower or reproduce, they must go through one of the following, depending on the plant:

1. Flooding
2. Wet-dry cycles
3. The death of the parent plant
4. Fire

You read that right: *fire*. The seeds that need fire to thrive come from (and grow into) *pyrophytic plants*. These plants require the intense heat of a wildfire to melt the resin that surrounds their seeds. Once burned, the plants can release their seeds and reproduce. But first, they must pass through the flames.

Sometimes the life we want and the character we crave come only by fire. Sometimes the process of growth begins only after certain parts of us have been set ablaze.

What wildfires have caused your becoming?

What wildfires are necessary to further your becoming?

I want to be able to pray with Randy Alcorn, who said, "Bring anything into my life — take anything away from my life as long as I get to be closer to you."[41] I'm not there yet, but I am moving closer, and I'm committed to faithfully becoming.

FAITHFUL TO AFFLICT

Whatever it takes. That's God's plan for your becoming. Even affliction.

A man approached the pastor of my previous church after a Sunday service and started angrily correcting him. My pastor had just taught out of the book of Job, and this man was furious that my pastor had said God afflicted Job. "God never does that" was this man's position.

Elsewhere in Scripture, though, David seems pretty sure that affliction is a part of God's toolbox for growing His followers. David says in Psalm 119:75, "I know, O LORD, that your rules are righteous, and that in faithfulness you have afflicted me."

Though it is true that God afflicts those He loves, He does not do it because He longs for our pain. Dane Ortlund, in his book *Gentle and Lowly*, does a remarkable job unpacking Lamentations 3:33, which says that God "does not afflict from his heart." Ortlund shares,

> The one who rules and ordains all things brings affliction into our lives with a certain divine reluctance. He is not reluctant about the ultimate

> good that is going to be brought about through that pain; that indeed is why he is doing it. But something recoils within him in sending that affliction. The pain itself does not reflect his heart.[42]

I remember waking up at 3 a.m. and wrestling with these truths during one of the most challenging seasons of my life. As I lay in bed, I would say over and over to myself the truths about God that I knew in my head but was struggling to believe in my heart: "Infinitely wise. Constantly good. Endlessly loving. Infinitely wise. Constantly good. Endlessly loving."

God's heart was not reflected in the affliction. It was reflected in me when He used the affliction to make me trust Him more.

God's heart is for His people. When we are in the middle of affliction, we can be tempted to doubt that. But the other side of the affliction always reveals a grander narrative. See the psalmist's testimonies:

> This is my comfort in my affliction, that your promise gives me life. (Psalm 119:50)
>
> Before I was afflicted I went astray, but now I keep your word. (Psalm 119:67)
>
> It is good for me that I was afflicted, that I might learn your statutes. (Psalm 119:71)

These verses are all from a *single* psalm. There is *always* a purpose in the affliction and challenges God brings you through.

I was reminded of this lesson in a new way when we had to fire someone at PHOS who was really good at his job. He was an excellent programmer. At lunch with one of our business consultants, I was still questioning the decision, hours out from needing to drop the news on this team member.

"What should I do," I asked, "when I think that firing this person would be the exact wake-up call he needs to become the professional I know he is called to be?"

"If that's true," the consultant replied, "then you have only one option: you have to fire him."

Sometimes the hardest moments are God's plan to help us in our journey to becoming.

In the midst of our own affliction, we must remain fully aware that we have a faithful God by our side and His ever-present Spirit living within us, even amidst the most challenging storms.

BECOMING > ACHIEVING

One of my closest friends started a physical therapy business that he ran for four years. This boy was a grinder. He was always working on the next thing to drive more interest and capture leads. He invested himself in content generation, networking events, and strategic partnerships, and he regularly developed new product offerings until he realized he just couldn't make it work.

When he decided to shut down the business and take a position with another company, I asked him how he was processing the closing of his business. He told me he felt like a failure. I sympathized with him and asked, "Okay, but what lessons did you learn? Who did you become over the past four years?"

He told me how he now better understands his strengths, passions, and joys, and how this journey had compelled him to confront and address those fundamental questions.

So, I asked him, "Then, was it really all a failure?"

What if success or failure isn't defined by whether we accomplish our goal, reach a target, or even see something through to the end but by who we are becoming in pursuit of the things we want?

We could work furiously on a new project, a new business venture, or a new personal goal, fail to achieve the results we want, and those things could still be a success in the Lord's eyes. But we could also work diligently on a new project, a new business venture, or a new personal goal, achieve all the results we want, and still be a failure in the Lord's eyes. The question is not *Did you achieve the right results?* but *Did your conduct and character honor the Lord in the middle of the work?*

When results are our focus, who we are becoming is unimportant to us. With outcome-based thinking, if we need something done, we just go get it done regardless of the costs or consequences. With a faithfulness mindset, we first ask if our plans align with God's plan, then we make room along the way to learn from the journey.

While your earthly pursuit may or may not yield the desired outcomes, choosing faithfulness is always fruitful. You might not see that fruit on your bank statement, though; it might just be in *you*.

Leader, untether yourself from the weight of outcome-based thinking that defines every one of your pursuits as a success or a failure based solely on your results. Submit yourself, instead, to a journey of learning and growing. The pursuit of becoming is a lifelong commitment; we'll never truly arrive. But it is through this journey that we cultivate deep faithfulness that honors God. As Martin Luther wrote,

> This life, therefore, is not righteousness, but growth in righteousness, not health, but healing, not being, but becoming. . . . We are not yet what we shall be, but we are growing toward it. The process is not yet finished, but it is going on. This is not the end, but it is the road. All does not yet gleam in glory, but all is being purified.[43]

The faithful leader's coffee mug reads "WORK IN PROGRESS," and faithful leaders are okay with that because they know it's God who is at work in them. He's at work in you. He's not finished yet, but He has promised He won't stop that work until He brings it "to completion at the day of Jesus Christ" (Philippians 1:6). Be faithful in your becoming.

FAITHFUL LEADER COMMITMENTS

01 In my becoming, I will embrace a mindset of constant reformation.

02 In my becoming, I will recognize the need to be cautious with the promises I make, being willing to unmake a promise when it no longer serves the best interests of those I lead.

03 In my becoming, I will prioritize character development over mere productivity.

04 In my becoming, I will trust God's plan and timing, knowing that He is shaping me for His purposes.

05 In my becoming, I will allow challenges and pressures to strengthen my resolve, character, and leadership abilities.

7

STEWARDSHIP

I judge all things only by the price they shall gain in eternity.[44]
JOHN WESLEY

SIX YEARS INTO my leadership role at PHOS, I found myself increasingly lonely. I was leading a monthly mastermind group for our local chamber of commerce, but I had a vision for something bigger: a group that would explore not just great leadership but *faithful* leadership. I wanted a group that could go deep on God's calling for our businesses.

In that season, Bob Shallow (my C12 Business Forum chair) reached out to me via LinkedIn to see if he could take me out to lunch to talk about my story and what he did. I took a cursory look at his LinkedIn profile, saw words like "purpose" and "leadership," and thought, *Free lunch with someone who loves leadership!? No question. Thumbs up.*

Over lunch, Bob asked me to talk about the things God was doing in my life, and I shared with him the vision that I had to start a Christ-centered mastermind group. I told him my dream was for the group to meet once a month and go deep on business strategy, accountability, and our biblical calling to lead. He asked me humbly, "Do you know what I do?"

You know those embarrassing networking moments where you realize you probably should have done some more preliminary research on the person you were meeting with? This was one of those moments.

"A little. Tell me more," I said with feigned confidence.

He informed me that he was full-time engaged in the activities I had just described with an organization called C12, headquartered in Texas. Bob shared that he was starting another forum in our area—adding to the hundreds of C12 forums that were already meeting each month around the nation—and he invited me to the first meeting.

A few weeks later, I attended the inaugural meeting for C12 Ocala, not knowing what to expect.

After opening with prayer and a time of self-reflection mixed with personal assessment, the day started with a devotional entitled "Spreading News of Great Joy: Commissioned to Speak Life." That's all it took for me to realize this was going to be a radically different business experience than I was used to for "corporate training."

As the day continued, we discussed a business management curriculum segment focused on building a customer service experience that reflected the gospel. I had heard a lot of customer experience talks before, but never had they explored a gospel application.

In the afternoon session, we conducted a self-assessment to identify the sinful thoughts and patterns in our lives that were impeding our leadership and limiting the potential ministry opportunities within our businesses.

I was floored. This group was exactly what I had been dreaming of.

At the end of the meeting, I went up to Bob and told him, "I want in. Can I lead one of these forums in Gainesville?"

"To lead a forum, you have to be a full-time chair," Bob said. That is, I'd have to stop managing PHOS.

"Got it—well, *not* leading one sounds great then," I said, and I signed up the next day to join C12 as a member.

Throughout my growing tenure in C12, I have been increasingly challenged by this one, central maxim of C12: your business is God's business; you are simply a steward.

> **Steward:** a person who is entrusted with responsibility and authority by an owner to look after his or her property in the owner's best interest

Stewardship is a profound calling for the faithful leader. It requires a deep level of yielding that results in a moment-by-moment question of "What do you want me to do next, God?" It's an awareness that everything we have we were given and entrusted with for a greater purpose than "me." Our authority, our resources, our influence, our businesses, and our families are all entrusted to us and are to be faithfully leveraged for God's purposes.

It's a different mindset, and it changes everything.

A NEW BUSINESS MODEL

Since the beginning of my entrepreneurship journey, I have been taught that there are two types of businesses an entrepreneur can build:

1. **A Lifestyle Business:** a business in which the operations, processes, organizational chart, and revenue model are structured in such a way that the founder (or the whole executive leadership team) can have the freedom to live life however they want with little regard for the actual company (e.g., pursuing hobbies all day)

2. **An Equity Business:** a business in which the organizational focus is on growth to secure a high valuation in order to sell the business for big multiples

While neither of these business models is necessarily wrong, I've found that they're simply insufficient for the faithful leaders seeking to steward their businesses for the glory of God.

It was C12 that first introduced me to a better organizational model for leading a company or team: **Business as a Ministry (BaaM)**.

Since PHOS' inception, I have run the company for the glory of God. I wanted God to be honored with the work we did and how we did it. But the more I learned about Business as a Ministry, I realized that God wanted to be glorified at PHOS not just in operational and service excellence but in and through Kingdom-oriented ministry that emanated from within PHOS.

As I began to hear stories of how other BaaM leaders were exporting gospel-centered, care-focused ministry from their businesses, I realized PHOS' operations were pretty far from this model. I was struck by stories of company prayer huddles, paid marriage seminars for employees, foster and adoption support programs, home-buying programs, corporate chaplaincy, company devotionals, faith-based financial management courses, mentorship and discipleship programs, and radical corporate generosity.

This was a different level of business stewardship.

STEWARD(SHIFT)

In December 2020, the executive team at PHOS hosted our two-day annual strategic planning session in Orlando. One of our annual planning rhythms is to write an annual primary objective for the year, the one big banner we can fly over the year. This is always really hard for me as a visionary leader. *How in the world am I supposed to choose 1 thing when I have 50 things for the next year?*

That year, we invited Bob Shallow to our meeting to help facilitate the first day of planning. When the time came for us to work on our annual primary objective, I took the chance to share with my team an idea I had been working on for months.

As we unpacked my vision, Bob eventually entered the conversation, stopped the discussion, and asked me a question: "If Jesus walked in right now and said that He would multiply tenfold the fruit of any initiative in your business, which organizational button would you want Him to press?"

I immediately said, "Our ministry impact."

Though I answered quickly and confidently, I was taken aback and challenged by the question. If the thing PHOS cared most about was scaling our impact, why wouldn't we set our annual primary objective on that target?

After a long debate and several iterations, we had our annual primary objective for the next year: "Operationalizing business as a ministry." We wanted every fiber of PHOS to reflect our commitment to business as a ministry. For the entire year, we examined how our revenue generation, operations management, organizational development, and financial management all reflected our stewardship of a BaaM philosophy.

Near the end of the next year, my friend and I enjoyed some tacos together as I celebrated with him some of the impact we had made that year by actively pursuing our objective. As I shared, he had a surprised look on his face. When I asked why, he told me, "I just can't believe you'd be willing to spend so much time on these initiatives. You could have been doing things to build your business."

His presupposition (that many of us naturally share) was that building a business primarily focused on anything other than market penetration and margin maximization isn't a worthwhile way to build a business.

Let's shift the perspective.

What if the reason God wants to bless a business is so that it can do more ministry? What if great business isn't just about stewardship of finances but about people and compassion? What if your faithfulness in leadership isn't defined by how much money you are able to generate but by how much care, love, and ministry you are able to export from the business?

The first two business models above don't ask these questions. They rest on the Friedman doctrine, also referred to as shareholder theory, which states that, "An entity's greatest responsibility lies in the satisfaction of the shareholders."[45] The theory suggests that a business that increases its revenues but does not increase its value to its shareholders does not fulfill its social responsibility.

It's an effective theory. Countless business empires have been built upon it. But there's a bigger picture to consider.

By contrast, a BaaM measures success not merely by shareholder ROI but also by a business' faithfulness and effectiveness in ministering to people. From a BaaM perspective, we are forced to answer this question: Does achieving tenfold revenue growth without a corresponding increase in our ministry impact align with our vision for *faithful* leadership?

Mike Sharrow, CEO of C12, said it this way: "People are not means to financial success. Business and financial systems are means to human impact and eternal success. Our future balance sheet will only have asset classes of people and faithfulness."[46]

I've heard business leaders say before, "Business would be great if I didn't have to deal with people." What a tragedy. Business wouldn't be worthwhile if it didn't include people. Your love, care, and compassion for people are the point of your business. People aren't just potential pain generators; they are purpose fuelers.

If that sounds like hard work that you're going to need God's help for every day, then this solidifies BaaM as the model for faithful leaders. After all, **what is faithfulness but daily hard work entrusted to God**?

If you lead a business, a department, or a team, your commitment to faithfulness will require a different perspective on how you are called to steward. Your stewardship extends beyond fiscal responsibility and into the daily hard work of shepherding people.

GUARDING PURPOSE

If you have identified your purpose, mission, or *why* within your company, business unit, and/or personal life, your next most important objective is to protect the daily pursuit of that purpose.

We had an intern work for us once, and, after months of being on our team, we sat down to review some analytics with her. We showed her the results of her work and how it had impacted the client. She was blown away. She told us, "I had no idea that my work was having that type of impact."

I hated to hear that. She had worked for PHOS for months without understanding her purpose on the team!

If we don't help our people see how their work changes people's lives, pushes the needle on our mission, and contributes to something greater than themselves, they'll simply come in every day, bang on their keyboard for eight hours, clock out, sleep, and do it all over again. That kind of work isn't fulfilling, it's not meaningful, and it's not a compelling enough reason to get out of bed every day when times are tough.

But Brandon, you may be thinking, *by showing the intern the unseen outcome of her work, weren't you encouraging an outcomes-based mindset instead of a faithfulness mindset?*

The faithfulness mindset doesn't mean you don't pay attention to outcomes. It means you prioritize chasing the *right* outcomes (people, impact, and purpose). When our people are working from a faithfulness mindset, it causes work to overflow with meaning, because we are ultimately working at being faithful to God, who has declared our obedience meaningful.

This stands in stark contrast to the outcome-based mindset, which traps us into thinking that all the work we do every day is just about making the next buck, completing the next project, or driving top-line or bottom-line growth. The outcome-based mindset can blind our people from seeing the impact and purpose of their work on a daily basis.

Purpose and the prospect of making a life-changing impact are the keys that can unlock deeper engagement, buy-in, and meaning at work for your people.

The problem is that purpose leaks. It leaks when the organization's mission and values, which once fueled its passion and directed its endeavors, gradually recede from prominence and give way to pragmatism.

Email, CRMs, sales goals, action plans, schedules, and agendas all work hard to keep our plates full of things that matter for our teams. The most natural thing to do with those stacks of needs is to get to work without thinking about why we do what we do. Faithful leaders, then, must take it upon themselves to help guard purpose in the workplace.

Without a commitment to stewarding your organization's purpose, what inevitably happens is mission drift. When we are not disciplined in guarding our purpose, we will eventually lose it as it slowly leaks out of our organization.

If you asked every person in your company today, "What is our purpose?" how would they answer? Would they answer the way that you want them to answer?

FIVE LEVELS OF PURPOSE ENGAGEMENT

The reality is that, in every organization, people will have differing levels of buy-in to the organization's purpose, ranging from highly disengaged to highly engaged.

Purpose Opponents	Purpose Critics	Purpose Passives	Purpose Followers	Purpose Champions

◀ - - - - - - - • - - - - - - - - - - - - • - - - - - - - - - - - • - - - - - - - - - - - - - - • - - - - - - - - - - - - - • - - - - - ▶

HIGHLY DISENGAGED   HIGHLY ENGAGED

> **Purpose Opponents:** the people within your organization who actively challenge, resist, or work against your stated purpose, creating conflict and negatively influencing others, thus impeding the organization's cohesion and progress

Purpose Critics: the people within your organization who wonder why you talk so much about mission, spend so much time on culture, make significant charitable donations, and do free work for people, expressing doubt about the significance and value of these missional activities

Purpose Passives: the people within your organization who will prioritize their individual work and typically have limited engagement in purpose-driven initiatives

Purpose Followers: the people within your organization who not only align with your organization's purpose but also exhibit genuine enthusiasm for it

Purpose Champions: the exceptional people within your organization who exemplify and promote the organization's purpose, inspiring others to do the same through their actions, advocacy, and the creation of a purpose-driven culture

In stewarding your organization's purpose, you should seek to move people further up the ladder by empowering your champions to pull team members deeper into your organization's purpose and terminating your active purpose opponents.

If you have a purpose worth working for, you have a purpose worth guarding. And with purpose, vision, and mission leaking uncontrollably out of your organization, guarding purpose has to start with you. To protect against mission drift and purpose fatigue, you must model faithful stewardship of organizational purpose by repeating, celebrating, and promoting your purpose every time you get an opportunity.

IT'S ALL YOURS, GOD

One way we promote faithful stewardship at PHOS is by reminding each other that each of us has our whole LIFE to give away. This acronym reminds us that we are intended to steward not just our money but our . . .

[L]abor

[I]nfluence

[F]inances

[E]xpertise

In every season of life, I've found different levels of resources available to me in each of these four areas.

I tend to think that when I have less financial resources available that I have nothing I can give away and that my responsibility for stewardship has been temporarily furloughed.

But faithful leadership isn't just about how we steward our finances. Everything we've been given has been entrusted to us to leverage for Kingdom purposes. David Platt reminds us what will matter to us at the end of our lives.

> We will not wish we had made more money, acquired more stuff, lived more comfortably, taken more vacations, watched more television, pursued greater retirement, or been more successful in the eyes of this world. Instead, we will wish we had given more of ourselves to living for the day when every nation, tribe, people, and language will bow around the throne and sing the praises of the Savior who delights in radical obedience and the God who deserves eternal worship.[47]

The question is not *What have you accomplished?* but *Have you been faithful with everything you have been entrusted with?* That is the central question a faithful steward asks.

ENTRUSTED WITH AUTHORITY

The opposite of a faithful steward is one who uses or abuses the influence entrusted to them for selfish gain. We find one in 3 John, which is one of those short, one-chapter books in the Bible. You can read through the whole book in 60 seconds.

Within John's 15 verses, we are introduced to two categories of people: faithful Christians whom John calls his "children," and a tyrant named Diotrephes, who is mentioned only in this book of the Bible.

In verses 5–8, John commends several fellow leaders whom he serves alongside. These individuals exemplify faithfulness by extending hospitality to strangers, commissioning other devoted leaders to spread the gospel, and fostering unity through their support of like-minded people.

Diotrephes, not so much.

> I have written something to the church, but Diotrephes, who likes to put himself first, does not acknowledge our authority. So if I come, I will bring up what he is doing, talking wicked nonsense against us. And not content with that, he refuses to welcome the brothers, and also stops those who want to and puts them out of the church. (3 John 9–10)

Diotrephes loved the spotlight, and any challenge to his prominence was viewed as a direct personal threat. He was leveraging his influence and authority to surround himself with yes-men who wouldn't question him, and he refused to welcome new people into the fellowship. On top of that, to maintain his position of authority, he used his platform to subtly belittle the other leaders around him, making them look foolish and incorrect so he could maintain his position of authority.

Utilizing his position of authority and influence, Diotrephes actively disregarded and dismissed the teachings of the appointed leaders in the church, even the apostles. He resorted to slandering these leaders both publicly and privately, while also excommunicating those who dared to oppose him.

It's easy to point fingers in stories about evil leaders like Diotrephes and think, *How could they!?* But let's point the finger back at ourselves for a moment.

For confident, bold leaders, it's easy for us to think we're always right and not invite new voices into the room. For capable, experienced leaders, it can be hard for us to share our leadership and learn to see our success not in our position, calling, or role but in the entrusting of our authority to new leaders.

How are you using the authority and influence entrusted to you? Do you use your authority to put yourself first in a conversation or decision-making process? How often do you publicly recognize other leaders on your team?

How do you deal with people who disagree with you? Are they a hindrance, impediment, or road bump to getting your plan accomplished? Do you try to remove them from the situation so you can see your agenda to completion, or do you value and invite even dissenting opinions so you can grow, learn, and be challenged?

God has granted us the authority we have, and we must guard and leverage it faithfully. Our authority was given to us for a greater purpose. We see this modeled in Peter's instruction to the church:

> Shepherd the flock of God that is among you, exercising oversight, not under compulsion, but willingly, as God would have you; not for shameful gain, but eagerly; not domineering over those in your charge, but being examples to the flock. . . . Clothe yourselves, all of you, with humility toward one another, for "God opposes the proud but gives grace to the humble." (1 Peter 5:2–5)

Instead of leveraging our authority to point other people to our own greatness or exploiting it for personal gain, we can use our position and influence to shepherd people and point them to God. We can pray in team meetings, we can celebrate the strengths of those we work with, and we can show other people where we see God at work in their lives.

The faithful steward seeks to use their resources to highlight God's greatness, not their own.

A MODERN-DAY DIOTREPHES

Unfortunately, many like Diotrephes are still walking this earth. Our sales team once had a great phone call with a man (we'll call him Jim) who was acting as a consultant managing the marketing for a potential client. During our discovery session with him, a blemish in the company's history surfaced, affecting its public perception: the owner had been in a tax fraud situation that cost millions to settle and had spent a year in prison.

During the next week, I took time to seek counsel on the best course of action. I also reached out to fellow business owners in their industry to gather their insights on the company owner's character. When I met with Jim again, I told him that I needed reassurance that the company had moved on from its past issues and that the owner had truly turned over a new leaf. He assured me, "We've changed everything since then. The owner is a different person."

My team and I thought it over, and, in the end, we chose to use this as an opportunity to demonstrate grace toward someone who had changed.

We started the project, and, after two months of building out and launching new campaigns for the client (and not yet receiving payment on any outstanding invoices), the owner wanted to sit down with us and discuss our results up to that point. I had been warned that his overall persona and character were intense, but we had worked with a lot of business owners in similar industries, and we were used to rough-skinned personalities. He came with two other managers from his staff and Jim, our point of contact.

I have never experienced anything like what I experienced in this meeting for the next 50 minutes.

We sat down at the conference table, and, as I began to open with a warm welcome and a moment for building rapport, I was interrupted with a loud, "Let me tell you what I'm here for . . ." The owner's 10-minute diatribe about his expectations made it clear he hadn't read through any of the materials we had provided for the past eight weeks, and it ended with a simple and rude request: "Respond to that."

In an effort to invite love back into the room, I took a big breath and responded collectedly, "Well . . . welcome to the studio! We are glad you are here and that we could finally meet together in person."

The meeting taught my team a valuable lesson, not only because of how we were treated but also in witnessing how the business owner treated others in the room. Jim was disrespected, degraded, and argued with, and, at one point during the meeting, the owner simply shouted, "Jim, Tom, I need to speak with you . . . outside!" as he stood up and stormed out the door.

The owner saw himself not as a steward but as a sovereign who believed that people were blessed just to work for him and that his demands should be met without question. While we had hoped to see a transformed person sitting in our studio, it became evident that this Diotrephes was still very much rooted in his old ways, wielding power with a heavy hand and with a disregard for humility, empathy, and respect for those entrusted to him.

By the world's standards, this owner had been mega successful. He had generated hundreds of millions in revenue over the tenure of his ownership. Somehow he even had 30 to 40 people willingly work for him at the time. But, after the meeting, my biggest takeaway was a reminder that you can be wildly successful in the world's eyes and be a total failure in God's eyes.

That's a sobering reality.

You could one day look back on your life and leadership and say, "A+." Others could look at it and say, "A+." And God could say, "F. Failure."

After the meeting, we collectively agreed to fire the client, canceling a contract worth the salary of two team members at PHOS. And, though we were promised during the meeting that we would be paid for the work we'd done, we never received any payments from the client.

In our final email to the client, I shared James 5:4: "Behold, the wages of the laborers who mowed your fields, which you kept back by fraud, are crying out against you, and the cries of the harvesters have reached the ears of the Lord of hosts."

This modern-day Diotrephes leveraged his authority to manipulate and control people, coerce them and instill fear, then gaslight anyone who disagreed with him. These are evil uses of entrusted authority.

The mindset of a faithful steward offers a better way to lead. As stewards, we recognize our authority is not our own. It is instead a temporary assignment of power entrusted to us for the good of other people and the glory of God. Your authority isn't a tool for you to generate wealth, build a reputation, or make your way into the spotlight. Your authority isn't for you.

Faithful leaders steward their authority to serve people, model loving leadership, and point people to the ultimate authority. Your people should feel safe around you, protected by your commitment to faithful stewardship.

You may even find that those outside your organization are drawn to the safety of your faithful stewardship. Jim, the consultant working for our former client, eventually quit the company because of what he experienced during our meeting. Months later, Jim was in a dark place and reached out to me personally for help because of how my team had responded. We were able to meet some personal needs he had and create an opportunity to model the gospel and point him to Christ. Those kinds of opportunities to influence others only come through faithful stewardship.

START AT HOME

Stewardship isn't just for the workplace. It actually starts at home.

Why is it often easier to give ourselves effortlessly and wholeheartedly to our jobs, careers, and the organizations we lead instead of to our homes? For one, the outcome-based mindset compels us to chase the results more easily achieved in the business environment than at home. But I also think we favor workplace stewardship over domestic stewardship because of the nature of the feedback we receive from each of these two domains.

A friend told me that leaders look into two mirrors every morning when they wake up: one for work and one for their home or family. Every morning, we ask the mirrors, "Mirror, mirror on the wall, who's the fairest of them all?" And we run to whichever mirror says back to us the loudest, "You're beautiful. You're an amazing leader. You're so valued."

We run to work when it tells us, "You're doing a great job," "I grow so much under your leadership," and "We are flourishing because of your influence." Meanwhile, home could be telling us, "Hey, you forgot to take out the garbage again," "Why didn't you help Sam study? He got an F on his exam," or "I don't feel loved. Where have you been?"

Which mirror are you running toward? My faithfulness is eroded every time I begin to run toward the first mirror and forget the second. I love the results and outcomes that come with influence, leadership, and success, and I find myself being lulled away from faithfulness at home by the outcome-based mindset and the praise of others.

If you are married and/or have children, they are your number one stewardship priority. *This* is where purpose and faithfulness start for you.

Since the day I started PHOS, I've maintained this commitment: "I will shut down PHOS before I ever let it destroy my marriage and/or my parenting."

Your business can always grow more. At the end of every day, there is always another contract you could have pursued, another acquisition you could have reviewed, or another networking event you could have attended. The opportunities are endless. But if giving 100% at work means you can only give 10% when you get home, then give less at work. *Your business, job, or ministry doesn't deserve your family.*

TRACKING FAITHFULNESS

All this talk about framing stewardship within a faithfulness mindset instead of an outcome-based mindset raises a tense question: why track anything? My friend Kevin once asked me this question point-blank.

On a walk with some men from my church one evening, I was sharing about the faithfulness mindset, and Kevin turned to me and asked, "So, do you guys track KPIs [key performance indicators] at PHOS then?"

This is truly the fundamental question at hand in this conversation about an outcome-based mindset versus a faithfulness mindset. What Kevin was asking was, "If you are emotionally abandoned to the outcome, if you surrender your results to God, and if you define success differently than whether you hit your goals, should you bother keeping track of any metrics? And if you do track metrics, why?"

I responded to Kevin, "We absolutely track metrics at PHOS. We have scorecards full of KPIs that we measure on a weekly basis. But our success is not contingent upon whether we meet these targets. Instead, our goal is to be faithful to the things God has called us to, regardless of the outcomes we achieve."

The faithful leader is even more persuaded than the outcome-based leader to track metrics, review KPIs, and hold people accountable. They are persuaded to do so not because they tie their definition of success to achieving all their goals but because of a deep commitment to honor Christ in their leadership. Our call to guard and grow all that we've been entrusted with is the thing that most compellingly demands our faithful stewardship of key performance metrics within our businesses or teams.

Outcome-based leaders measure every metric they can because they want to ensure they produce something impressive and have something to show for all the hard work they've put in.

Faithful leaders measure every metric they can because they want to steward their resources through supervision and reporting while being content to entrust and surrender the results to a faithful God.

William Carey, an English missionary, famously said, "Expect great things from God; attempt great things for God."[48]

Like Carey, faithful leaders will set their sights high, measure their KPIs diligently, aim for the best results, and even "expect great things from God." They will, however, simultaneously yield their hearts to a faithful, all-knowing, and all-powerful God, who may or may not bring about their targeted and planned-for results. They will be content regardless of the outcome, knowing they have fought the good fight, persevered in the race, and remained faithful to the end.

What key performance indicators could you begin to track to measure faithfulness in the stewardship of your business? What Kingdom-oriented KPIs would help you stay focused on leading your business, organization, team, or family faithfully based on the things that matter most to the Lord?

THANKFULLY, YOU ARE NOT GOD

One date night, Shelley and I were headed to Chili's when I began a minor emotional meltdown. (She says it was more than "minor.")

I had just returned from my first mission trip, and, after being away for two weeks, I had a lot to catch up on. When I got home, I discovered that one of my teenage kids was sick. So, to prevent my own illness, I had kept my distance from him for the past 48 hours. Unfortunately, this distance left him feeling hurt.

On our car ride to the restaurant, Shelley pointed out my son's frustration to me. My dramatic response went something like this: "We're in such a difficult season right now at work that if I get sick and can't make the meeting later this week, I could see PHOS closing."

Shelley sat quietly for a moment, then asked me, "What's something God has done for PHOS in the past? Where have you seen God be faithful to PHOS?"

I wasn't in the mood to play this game, but I didn't want to show how unspiritual I was being, so I responded with a short story.

Shelley nodded. "What's another story?"

Feeling annoyed but suspecting she would end the questioning soon, I reluctantly provided her with another story.

Relentlessly, she asked again, "What's another story?"

Now frustrated, I gave her a third story, then a fourth, and then a fifth. At that point, I had to cut her off, "How many times are you going to ask me this?"

"As many times as it takes for you to start trusting Jesus again," she replied.

Oof.

The outcomes-based mindset can lead us to dark places where we can't even see the faithful God we serve anymore. We think the results are completely in our hands and that if we don't act, the whole system is going to come crumbling down. Our spiritual amnesia sets in hard and we forget that it's God who is in control of our outcomes, guiding them as He pleases for our good and His glory. We get so caught up in controlling our outcomes and doing everything we can to make sure things go exactly the way we want them that we lose ourselves.

You are simply a steward. This is a freeing reality that reminds us that God is in control of our lives and leadership. We need only to faithfully steward the resources, people, influence, and businesses that have been assigned to us, starting at home.

FAITHFUL LEADER COMMITMENTS

01 As a steward, I commit to evaluating every opportunity based on its eternal value.

02 As a steward, I commit to embracing a business model that leverages my platform for a purpose bigger than profit.

03 As a steward, I commit to leveraging my authority and resources to serve and point others to God.

04 As a steward, I commit to defining and guarding a purpose at work that is worth working for.

05 As a steward, I commit to prioritizing my family and home as my first responsibility.

06 As a steward, I commit to tracking faithfulness through Kingdom-oriented key performance indicators (KPIs).

8

PERSEVERANCE

I pray to God to give me perseverance and to deign that I be a faithful witness to Him to the end of my life for my God.[49]

SAINT PATRICK

PICTURE THIS: It's 10:45 p.m., and it has been an exhausting day. Your schedule was full of back-to-back meetings, a big client just canceled their contract, a key member just announced they are resigning, and, to top it all off, you had to make an emergency trip to school to pick up your child because he was throwing up during snack time.

At 11 p.m., you are finally crawling into bed, but, as your head hits the pillow, one of your closest friends texts you that he is outside. Trusting that it must be important, you head downstairs, open the door, and find him with a huge smile on his face.

He tells you that your favorite store, the one you love to shop at (Best Buy, Loft, REI, etc.), is going out of business, and they are giving away everything they have for free. They just made the public announcement, so not many people know about it, and the offer ends at midnight.

Even in your exhausted, zombie-like state, I suspect that you'd somehow find the energy to put on your shoes and head out with your friend. Why? Because it's easy to do something when you are excited about the outcome. You wouldn't think of the time you'd give up and the sleep you'd lose as a sacrifice.

But what if, instead of a text from your friend, your spouse rolled over right as you were climbing into bed and said, "Babe, you're going to hate me, but I just remembered about Little Kimmy's class party tomorrow. We signed up to bring three dozen of Grandma's famous cupcakes."

That moment would require sacrifice.

Faithfulness is about making those sacrifices. It's about persevering to do hard things you don't want to do. Maybe for you the hard thing is . . .

1. A team member you know you need to let go
2. A phone call you know you need to make
3. A board of directors you know you need to resign from
4. A project you know you need to start

No matter what the hard thing is you're facing, you're called to persevere and make the sacrifice God is calling you to.

Perseverance is a way of life for faithful leaders, even in the face of pressure and uncertain outcomes. Regardless of their fear, discomfort, and stress, faithful leaders continue forward, pressing on resolutely into the storm.

ANYWAY

In Austin Channing Brown's book *I'm Still Here: Black Dignity in a World Made for Whiteness*, she explains why her black American parents gave her the name of a white male. In their estimation, the name "Austin Brown" would help to ensure that her future career opportunities would be as plentiful as those of any white, male American applicant.

The book is a raw, honest look at how a black woman operates inside a world she argues is "made for whiteness." For most of the book, Brown shares understandable frustrations about systems, presuppositions, and practices that tend to favor white individuals by offering them greater opportunities.

When questioned about where she finds hope amidst the struggles and her efforts to educate America, Brown offers a beautiful perspective on faithfulness:

> [My hope] is but a shadow. It is working in the dark, not knowing if anything I do will ever make a difference. It is speaking anyway, writing anyway, loving anyway. It is enduring disappointment and then getting back to work. It is knowing this book may be read only by my Momma, and writing it anyway. It is pushing back, even though my words will never be big enough, powerful enough, weighty enough to change everything. It is knowing that God is God and I am not.[50]

I love Brown's repetition of the word *anyway*. That word is pulled from the lexicon of faithful leaders. One thing we can't determine is whether all the effort we put in will actually pay off in the end. The faithful leader does what is right *anyway*.

What if your extra degree, additional certifications, and added courses don't land you that new opportunity you hoped for? Faithful leaders move forward anyway.

What if you commit to investing in your marriage, dating your spouse more regularly, and inviting love back into your home, but your spouse doesn't reciprocate? Faithful leaders persevere anyway.

What if you pour yourself into this new culture initiative at work, outlining all the plans, creating all the engagement pizzazz, showing your team exactly how the new program is going to change their life, and only two people sign up? Faithful leaders follow through anyway.

What if you invest all this money into therapy, counseling, and groups only for your brother or sister or mother or father to relapse and end up back in the hospital . . . again? Faithful leaders sacrifice anyway.

Everything faithfulness requires of us, it requires without any promise of an earthly return on investment. Faithful leaders content themselves with doing the right thing, even though they have no guarantee it will ever yield the results they are hoping for.

In other words, they pull a William Carey.

During Carey's missionary work in India in the early 1800s, he was able to have the Bible translated into multiple Indian dialects for the first time in history. Despite his unwavering commitment, Carey did not witness a single conversion during his 35 years of ministry.[51] Even though he didn't see the fruits of his labor, he kept on anyway. Carey persevered, even without a promised outcome, because he knew this pleased God. John MacArthur shares about Carey, "Some people think he had a fruitless ministry. But almost every convert in India to this day is fruit on his branch, because he translated the New Testament into many different Indian dialects. Carey was not the one to directly reap what he had sown, but his life bore much fruit."

Faithful leader, the fruit of your labor is often unseen. The vast majority of the fruit of your faithfulness you will never see. Sometimes when you share a story or an encouragement with someone, they'll wind up sharing that story with someone else, who will then share it with someone else, and it will wind up changing that person's life. You'll probably never hear those stories, but you share and lead anyway.

That's the heart of a faithful, persevering leader.

WITHOUT RECIPROCATION

One of the clearest pictures of persevering faithfulness that God has given us is in marriage.

During college, I went to the strangest bachelor party I have ever been invited to. The groom, my best friend, didn't want us to plan the party. He already had the vision and wanted us to simply execute that vision.

He asked that we gather 15 to 20 of his closest friends into his living room and spend two to three hours sharing our best Bible-centered marriage advice. That party is, still today, one of my all-time favorite dude-gathering memories.

In chairs circled around the room, we swapped verses and marital learning lessons. When it was my turn, I flipped to Ephesians 5 and exhorted my friend to love his wife as Christ loved the church. With a few years of marriage already under my belt, I shared with him the best wisdom I had collected:

> Friend, you are too new in your relationship to understand this, but, one day, you and your wife will struggle to love each other. It may be for a moment or for a season, but your honeymoon phase will soon end, and love for your wife will become what it is in every other relationship in your life: an intentional commitment you make that takes discipline, energy, and time.
>
> For some of those seasons, you may even feel like some of that work is highly one way: you're giving, you're investing, and you're loving, but you're not getting anything back. In other seasons, your wife will feel the same.
>
> In an effort to love your wife as Christ loved the church, I want to encourage you to keep loving her in those moments. Keep loving your wife even when it feels unreciprocated.

You are never more like Jesus than when you are loving someone who is not loving you in return. That is gospel love.

My gift to my friend at this bachelor party was a reminder that faithful, persevering love keeps going even when it's not returned. When you love like that, be encouraged—you are acting just like your faithful Father.

When your kids are on their sixty-third meltdown today, keep loving anyway.

When your employee is railing on you because he is struggling to balance work and a new, hard season in his personal life, keep loving anyway.

When your spouse is struggling with depression and you feel like it's been a while since he or she actively invested in you or the relationship, keep loving anyway.

Faithfulness is calling us to view success in these moments as staying true to our commitment to persevering love. When we love despite these challenges, we reflect the unconditional love of our Father. May people be able to say over us, "The steadfast love of Brandon [or your name] never ceases. It is a faithful and sure thing."

Faithful leaders don't have to receive in order to give. They persevere in love even without reciprocation. We'll never regret giving ourselves to that type of love.

> Love is never wasted, for its value does not rest upon reciprocity.[52]

NO ENDURING RELATIONSHIPS WITHOUT FORGIVENESS

God designed marriage as a living picture of Christ's persevering love for His bride, the church. Sadly, spouses don't always represent God's perseverance and faithfulness well.

More than 10 years into his marriage, Alexander Hamilton had an affair. The resulting wake of his infidelity was wide and brutal. He was manipulated by the adulteress' husband to pay regular fines in order to keep the secret quiet. However, when this arrangement was exposed, his financial transactions prompted some to accuse Hamilton of misusing government funds in connection to the affair. This scandal had the potential to jeopardize not only his career but also the future of the Federalist Party itself.

To exonerate himself, Hamilton penned a document entitled the "Reynolds Pamphlet," which detailed his marital betrayal and the technicalities of his affair. In doing so, he brought public shame upon himself and his family, and he officially opened the floodgates to a world of unimaginable pain and sorrow for Eliza, his wife.

What is so powerful about the story presented in *Hamilton* is Eliza's faithfulness. My wife loves to say that Eliza is the real hero of the story.

In the most emotionally impactful part of the entire performance, Alexander and Eliza walk through a garden holding hands as the choir sings about the grace of forgiveness—a grace powerful enough to push even the worst offenses permanently behind us. The choir asks rhetorically, "Forgiveness, can you imagine?"

That's a picture of persevering love. The kind spouses should have for each other. The kind God has for us. As the psalmist David wrote, "As far as the east is from the west, so far does he remove our transgressions from us" (Psalm 103:12).

After Alexander was shot and killed by Aaron Burr, Eliza continued steadfastly in her faithfulness. In 1806, Eliza founded the first private orphanage in New York, honoring Alexander's orphanhood. She spent her time combing through copious amounts of writings by Alexander, publicizing his work for the world, and laboring to tell his story.

Eliza's forgiveness is a true demonstration of faithful love, "a grace too powerful to name," as her song with Alexander calls it. It is a commitment to do the hard, undeserved, right thing. She was faithful despite his unfaithfulness; a beautiful picture of the gospel.

There are no enduring relationships without forgiveness. None. It doesn't have to be infidelity that threatens to tear apart relationships. It can be differences of opinion, preferences, disagreements, arguments, misunderstandings, or conflicting priorities. Perseverance calls us to keep loving even when someone fails us. It won't be long before we find ourselves in need of the same forgiveness, so we ought to be the first to give it.

As Lewis writes, "To be a Christian means to forgive the inexcusable, because God has forgiven the inexcusable in you."[53] True forgiveness is impossible without Christ in us. But because God has forgiven us and is working to make us more like Himself, we are able to look beyond the failures of others and find ways to love them despite the pain they have caused us.

While faithful leadership calls us to persevering love, it does not imply that we should endure abusive and exploitative relationships. In fact, true faithful leadership involves fighting for justice and advocating for the vulnerable and oppressed. If you find yourself in such a situation, your perseverance requires you to fight for justice, both for yourself and others who may be affected while you extend forgiveness.

No matter the situation, faithful leadership calls us to persevere, to love, and to do what is right, regardless of the outcome.

THE ENDLESS SEA OF OPINIONS

Perseverance, by nature, involves conflict: conflict in our circumstances, within ourselves, or with others (or all three). One of the most fatiguing threats to faithfulness (requiring perseverance to overcome) is conflict with the opinions of people you care about and who care about you.

Shelley and I were married at 19. We got married in between our freshman and sophomore years at the University of Florida. At 21 years old, we announced to our parents we were pregnant with our first child. At the time, I was headed for pastoral ministry studying family, youth, and community sciences.

When we told Shelley's mom we were pregnant, she burst into tears. Not the "Wonderful! What a joy!" kind of tears. These were tears of "How could you ruin your life with a choice like this? You can't afford kids! You're going to live in Alabama with 10 kids in a shack!"

She clearly disagreed with our choice for Shelley to drop out of college and start our family so young, and she mourned our announcement for almost a week. (Eventually, my mother-in-law came around, though, and loved our children deeply.)

Not everyone is going to agree with the decisions you make. Who are you going to focus on pleasing? Mom? Dad? Boss? Jesus?

People will always have opinions, but those opinions won't always line up with what God wants for your life. I was reminded of this when I made a difficult financial decision for our family.

I started day trading in the stock market in my early 30s. My dad is a financial advisor for a Fortune 500 company and has always taught me about smart money management and the importance of saving and investing. Over time, a few stocks turned into a small portfolio that I was self-managing online alongside some cryptocurrency. It didn't take long until I was checking on these investments *all the time*. Between 2 and 20 times a day, I would check prices, watch news headlines, read financial blogs, set new alert notifications, and question, *Do I buy!?? Do I sell!??*

It became consuming. My conversations with friends and family began to revolve more and more around the stock market, and I felt a growing anxiety and pride welling in my heart. This newfound hobby was creating in me a love of money.

Not everybody struggles with this—I get it—but for me, day trading was creating an idol in my heart. *How do I get more money? Oh man, I just lost thousands! Oh yes, I just made thousands! Money!!!* I was becoming less concerned with generating profit at PHOS and more concerned with managing my distributed shareholder profit.

So I decided to make the hard decision. Even though some of the things I had invested in were performing well above my advisors' returns, I decided to sell all my investments and give my advisors all the control of the funds. It wasn't a decision I made for money; it was a decision I made for repentance.

Over the following weeks and months, I felt my heart slowly untether itself from my financial performance and fix itself back on love and leadership. My conversations slowly shifted away from dividends and back to discipleship.

My friends, on the other hand, thought this was a really dumb financial move, and they wanted to regularly let me know. They would send me text messages with screenshots that showed the performance of the stocks I had just sold out on. There would be little sarcastic, backhanded comments made at lunches about the huge payouts I had been missing since selling.

In those moments, caring more about God's opinion than my friends' opinions required the death of an outcome-based mindset ("I want/need/deserve more money") and a perseverance in living from a faithfulness mindset ("I need to give up anything that threatens my daily walk with Jesus").

Protecting my heart from the love of money required a hard decision. I knew when I made the decision I would be sacrificing returns. But I knew I was investing in a greater reward that God wants me to persevere toward. As Paul wrote to the church in Philippi,

> Indeed, I count everything as loss because of the surpassing worth of knowing Christ Jesus my Lord. For his sake I have suffered the loss of all things and count them as rubbish, in order that I may gain Christ and be found in him, not having a righteousness of my own that comes from the law, but that which comes through faith in Christ, the righteousness from God that depends on faith—that I may know him and the power of his resurrection, and may share his sufferings, becoming like him in his death, that by any means possible I may attain the resurrection from the dead. (Philippians 3:8–11)

Paul is saying that anything we give up is nothing compared to the value of knowing and being known by God.

In other words, perseverance is worth it.

When you make one of those hard, daily decisions to trust God, people will inevitably disagree with you, just as Job's friends disagreed with him. You'll be surrounded by a host of opinions that make you wonder, *Did I make the right decision?*

When you choose to dismiss a large client because they are toxic to your team . . .

"But they make us so much money!"

When you choose not to hire a job candidate with a great resume because she does not fit your culture . . .

"But they are the best at what they do!"

When you choose to overhaul a strategy, product line, or process because you've seen the numbers sliding . . .

"But we've always done it like this!"

When you choose to lay off a team member because your strategic plan no longer requires him . . .

"But they've worked here forever. They're family!"

Faithful leadership will require you to hold fast to hard and healthy decisions that you know are right, even when others disagree, don't see the wisdom, and question your motives.

Perseverance is standing ground in the endless sea of opinions. It's seeking counsel, abiding in Jesus, and making a wisdom-driven decision—then being faithful to follow through as the ripple effects begin to hit the shore, leaving your hands wide open with the Lord in case you're wrong.

JOYFUL, RESULTLESS RESOLVE

Allen Gardiner,[54] born in England in 1794, had a lifelong dream of becoming a sailor. His passion for seafaring was evident even in his youth, as he immersed himself in every adventure story he could find. He was once caught by his mother sleeping on the floor, driven by his determination to acclimate himself to the rugged lifestyle of a sailor.

He enrolled in the naval college at 14, was at sea by 16, and eventually became commander of the Royal Navy.

Later in life, God called Gardiner out of the navy to start his own missionary organization and use his naval skills to travel to South Africa and South America for mission work.

Throughout his missionary journeys, Gardiner endured the most extreme weather conditions, various illnesses, language deficiencies, hostile tribes, threats against his life, theft, robbery, isolation, loneliness, and a lack of resources, funding, food, clothing, and shelter.

He spent years trying to reach people in different countries, with every trip ending in some form of forced abandonment of the mission.

Along the way, Gardiner's mom, wife, and daughter all died. He was denied missionary rights because he wasn't ordained, and he was shut down by fierce tribal chieftains, government officials, and even church leaders, having been told at one point by the Protestant Dutch Government, "You might as well try to instruct the monkey as the natives of Papua. . . . Don't interfere with the natives; they'll never be any different."[55]

After years of failed efforts, the mission committee that had been supporting Gardiner was ready to abandon their work in South America. Nevertheless, Gardiner was able to recruit six men to make a trip back to Tierra del Fuego in Southern Patagonia. They brought four months' worth of supplies and a promise from England to renew their resources within that window.

They left in September 1850, sailing for months on wildly stormy seas before disembarking at Banner Cove, where they were left alone as their ship sailed back to England.

Despite an ingenious plan to safeguard their supplies in a tent surrounded by a thorny fence, the natives began to steal their provisions. Faced with the harsh weather conditions and depleting supplies, the missionaries were left with no option but to retreat to their last remaining small boat and live in the shallows and on the shore.

Back in England, Gardiner's supporters couldn't find a ship's crew willing to make the dangerous journey to bring Gardiner and his men the next six months' worth of supplies. And as Gardiner and his men spent months on the shore of Patagonia, only occasionally interacting with the locals, their food supply dwindled until it was gone.

By the time a relief ship finally reached Patagonia in October 1851, almost a year after the missionaries had arrived, Gardiner and his men had all died of starvation.

Nobody is going to make a movie about Allen Gardiner. Why? Because the people we love to tell stories about are the ones who accomplished big things and experienced fairy tale endings. What would the outcome-based mindset have to say about Allen Gardiner's life?

When Allen Gardiner's emaciated body was found lying beside his men on the beach of Tierra del Fuego, he was clothed in three layers with wool stockings over his arms to ward off the numbing cold. Next to their bodies, the British officers found Gardiner's personal journal. The last entry was in Gardiner's hand, written on September 6, 1851.

> I am happy day and night, hour by hour. Asleep or awake, I am happy beyond the poor compass of language to tell. My joys are with Him whose delights have always been with the sons of men. . . . As I day by day and night by night lie here, what a world, unknown to the world, do I live and have my thoughts, and move my affections in! God is indeed about my bed. . . . Let all my beloved ones at home rest assured that I was happy beyond expression the night I wrote these lines and would not have changed situations with any man living . . . [and] that heaven, and love, and Christ . . . were in my heart. . . . Much more could I add, but my fingers are aching with cold, and I must wrap them up in my clothes; but my heart, my heart is warm, warm with praise, thanksgiving, and love to God my Father, and love to God my Redeemer.[56]

Gardiner's faithful perseverance didn't yield the world's fruit, but it did yield the peaceful fruit of righteousness. His joy came not from his results but from his identity in Christ, his calling fulfilled, and his future hope in a life to come. Allen Gardiner's life was a life lived for Christ and for others, and, even in his dying moments, he wouldn't have changed his situation with any man. His faithful resolve had brought him joy in Jesus.

Our calling as faithful leaders is the same: daily hard work entrusted to God with a persevering and joyful resolve, regardless of our results.

LEADERSHIP HITS AND TACKLES

We may not have been chased out of the woods to starve on a boat for Jesus (at least not yet), but most of us have had to persevere through some harsh criticism.

One day, I asked a volunteer from our worship team to lunch so we could talk through how we could better serve one another on the team. Over some delicious tacos (yes, I eat a lot of tacos and, no, I'm not Mexican, I just wish I was), I started the conversation with one simple question: "Hey, so over the past nine months of working together, what have been some challenges that we can work on overcoming?"

I didn't know I had opened Pandora's Box and all evil was about to be released to the world.

For the next 25 minutes, I took notes silently while he shared every hurtful and brash thing he could think of: "We are thinking about leaving the church, but before we go, I want you to know I think you are a condescending, dismissive leader; a derelict father; and someone who should be disqualified from ministry."

Great meeting.

The thing with criticism is that there is always a little truth in it. When people are criticizing you, they're sharing their point of view, and that's valid. That's what makes it tough to handle hurtful criticism and figure out how to deal with it as a faithful leader.

Over the years, I have been mentored to respond to feedback with the following steps:

1. **Listen well.**

   What is true? Be willing to search your heart for patterns of sinful behavior that are consistent with the feedback. Ask the Lord to reveal any areas of spiritual weakness for which you need repentance and greater faith.

   > Search me, O God, and know my heart! Try me and know my thoughts! And see if there be any grievous way in me, and lead me in the way everlasting! (Psalm 139:23–24)

2. **Seek wisdom.**

   What do other people see? Can other people verify the accuracy or inaccuracy of the critique?

   > Where there is no guidance, a people falls, but in an abundance of counselors there is safety. (Proverbs 11:14)

3. **Consider the source.**

   Does the person who provided the feedback know you deeply? Is this person someone who is invested in your growth and willing to come alongside you to help you grow, or are they simply a backseat driver? Are they a hater or a loving friend?

   > Better is open rebuke than hidden love. Faithful are the wounds of a friend; profuse are the kisses of an enemy. (Proverbs 27:5–6)

4. **Grow and move on.**

   Take everything that is true and create a growth plan for intentional steps forward, surrounding yourself with people who will help you and hold you accountable. Once you've done that, move on. Don't get stuck in a cycle of shame or condemnation. Press on.

> Forgetting what lies behind and straining forward to what lies ahead, I press on toward the goal for the prize of the upward call of God in Christ Jesus. (Philippians 3:13–14)

Perseverance and faithful leadership call us to walk through these steps when we receive criticism. Though painful, I searched my heart and found the places where I needed to grow. I brought the feedback to several pastors in my life, who agreed these things were not true (not that there was nothing to learn, but that these did not describe my life). I considered the source (someone about to leave the church who was hurting, not someone who was sticking around to help people grow). I sought forgiveness for areas of sinful behavior, and I moved on.

It can be really hard to move on after someone rips you wide open. Their words can stick around in your heart and live rent-free in your head long after you first hear them.

The day after my meeting with the disgruntled church member, I texted the men in my community group asking for prayer. On my drive down to my morning meeting, I couldn't help but continue to process all the aggressive criticism I had received from the conversation. I was supposed to be listening to an audiobook in preparation for the meeting, but I couldn't focus, so I just drove in silence. Eventually, I decided to put on some music to focus my thoughts on the Lord, and I happened to put on a track from Cory Asbury called "Unraveling."[57] Asbury writes that, as he is being unraveled by the Lord,

> It's worse than I thought it would be
> But I've never been happier

God will use criticism to unravel you, squeeze out what is inside, reveal the hidden things of your heart, and challenge your commitment to faithfulness.

The unraveling is always much more painful than we expect it will be, but it makes us stronger. It makes us happier because it forces us to be faithful—to move forward with a greater hope and a greater sense of accomplishment in becoming and persevering—rather than leaving us to find our identity in the opinions of other people.

While I was listening to the song, a close friend from that group of men shot me a text message that immediately had me in tears:

> Love you, brother. Whatever was said to you yesterday, just know that you have been the most incredible friend and mentor to me over the last six years. The heart you have for the Lord and for others is amazing, and I am praying for you always, bro. Let me know if I can help.

If you haven't been through something similar, where someone rips your soul out of your chest, runs over it with a car several times, and then hands it back to you, you will eventually.

When those times come, you must keep going.

We could shut down; we could stop what we're doing; we could pull back, pull out, or give up, but that's not what leadership requires. That's not what our calling to faithful perseverance requires.

When you receive soul-crushing feedback, don't allow any root of bitterness to make its way into your heart and destroy you and your influence (Hebrews 12:15). Let it strengthen your character and resolve.

When you receive heart-wrenching criticism, don't try to step in front of the story, control the narrative, and subtly malign the other person in public (Romans 12:19). Entrust your reputation to God.

When you receive spirit-shattering comments, don't get sidetracked from your mission to pursue unity, love, and peace (2 Corinthians 13:11). Stay your post; this is what you signed up for as a leader.

The things that make leadership difficult are the very things that create the need for leaders worth following.

That is the mindset that faithfulness requires.

At a leadership conference I attended, Sadie Robertson Huff spoke briefly about her grandmother. A godly, wise woman, her grandmother would regularly tell Sadie, "If you're holding the football, you're going to get tackled. It's simple. It's just how it is."[58]

If you're in a leadership position, you're the one holding the football. Expect to get tackled, and persevere when it happens.

A BRUISED REED HE WILL NOT BREAK

One of the times I was tackled as a leader came when a client of PHOS, after years of working with us, requested that we create a series of new creative media pieces with content that contradicted our company's core beliefs. It was impossible for us to fulfill their requests with a clear conscience.

When we told the client that, they were *furious*.

We spent months meeting with them, explaining our genuine desire to continue the work we had done with them for years, focusing on a long list of things PHOS was able to continue doing for them. They were not interested.

In our final meeting with the client, I read the two representatives a seven-page document titled "PHOS' Statement of Faith" that we had drafted with the help of Alliance Defending Freedom, a leading faith-based nonprofit that focuses on legal advocacy for religious freedom.

When I finished reading the document, I was truly hopeful that they would see our heart for them and that this could be a reconciling moment for us.

After a long, very awkward pause, that hope vanished.

"PHOS is a platform for spreading hatred. I used to refer you a lot. I could never refer you again."

Due to the client's hostility, disrespect for my team, and their unwillingness to compromise, we were left with no choice but to terminate our partnership with them. After we sent that email, they responded simply with a vague note about moving forward with their "next steps."

For the next two months, I woke up every morning struggling with the worst anxiety I've ever dealt with. *Is today going to be the day I have a lawsuit sitting in my inbox? What if other clients hear about this? How is this going to affect our reputation in the community?*

I wrote this in my journal during that season:

> Fear is so debilitating. It makes you want to stop. To pause. To not move forward. To retreat. To be insular. To protect yourself. The question "What if?" is daunting.
>
> During this season, the Word is such a balm to me. I feel such a need for my dependence on God. He is my only rescue.
>
> What does peace look like during this season?
>
> I opened my Bible this morning and began to review what I had read last time. The first thing I read was this:
>
>> But the Lord said to him, "Go, for he is a chosen instrument of mine to carry my name before the Gentiles and kings and the children of Israel. For I will show him how much he must suffer for the sake of my name." (Acts 9:15–16)
>
> I read that and said to myself, "Dang it." [Though this passage was written specifically about the apostle Paul, I knew what God was calling me to do.]
>
> What if faithfulness means you willingly embracing God's desire to use you as a chosen instrument of suffering?

As a result of my uncertainty about what the client would do in response to our terminating the relationship, everything in me wanted to stop doing ministry for a season, get off the stage, go dark online, and pull my head back into the turtle shell to protect myself, my team, my family, and my church.

At some point in this season, I came across the aphorism "There is only one way to avoid criticism: do nothing, say nothing, and be nothing." I had two options:

Option #1: Do nothing, say nothing, be nothing (be safe).

Option #2: Keep doing the work of an evangelist, speaking the truth in love, and being steadfast in my calling (be faithful).

In our pursuit of faithful leadership, we will be called to suffer for the sake of the name of Jesus. When you're planning to scuba dive in the ocean and sharks start circling your boat, your only options are to abort the mission and steer back to shore or to follow the dive plan and trust your dive master. Those moments will test you emotionally and spiritually, but you are not alone. Persevere through your fear, let your light shine, and know that God will use your faithfulness.

> A bruised reed he will not break,
> and a faintly burning wick he will not quench. (Isaiah 42:3)

LEADING WITH A 104° FEVER

As leaders, we aren't always tackled by people's direct opposition. Sometimes we're tackled simply by the natural difficulties of life in a fallen world. One story of faithful perseverance in the midst of hardship sticks out to me from the 2022 Global Leadership Summit. At this GLS, I got to see a performance by Sara Evans, a decorated American country music artist. After her performance, the conference emcee pulled her aside to ask her some questions about leadership in front of the audience.

When asked about some of the challenging things she'd been through, Sara shared a story about a big concert she had booked in Australia. The night she was to perform in front of thousands of people on a big stage, she had a fever—but not just any fever. She had a 104°F fever. (I literally can't move with anything greater than 101°F.) What was she supposed to do? She was in Australia with a giant crowd that had paid in full.

Unbelievably, Sara got on stage that night and completed the set in full fever.

As I processed her decision, I realized this is what we do every day as a leader.

Single parents, you don't get home after a challenging workday and think, *I'm not really feeling it tonight, so I'm just going to need you to go and figure things out for yourself tonight, Mr. Four-Year-Old.*

Similarly, your business is most likely not in a place where you can just step away for a month while you go "get your life together."

No, each of us has some sort of fever we're regularly struggling with—physically, emotionally, spiritually, financially, relationally, occupationally, or a combination of a bunch of these things. And, in the middle of those plaguing 104°F+ fevers, we have to get on stage with our team, within our company, or with our family and continue to lead.

It was in the midst of grief that I first learned this lesson.

I don't think I really knew what grief was until my mom passed away. I remember a conversation with my wife in which I was explaining how I was feeling (emotionally exhausted, intellectually empty, and spiritually bankrupt), and she told me, "Yeah, you're grieving."

"No, you don't understand, sweetheart. I'm not, like, crying all the time," I responded.

"Yeah, you're grieving," she said sweetly.

"No, no, no," I clarified. "Again, when you leave the house, it's not like I sit here by myself in the dark and just cry."

I was grieving, and I didn't even know it. In the middle of my grief, I still had a team to lead, a company to run, and a family that needed to be loved.

C. S. Lewis, in his book *A Grief Observed*, shares his account of grappling with grief after his wife's passing: "No one ever told me that grief felt so like fear. I am not afraid, but the sensation is like being afraid. . . . At other times it feels like being mildly drunk, or concussed. There is a sort of invisible blanket between the world and me. I find it hard to take in what anyone says."[59]

Regularly, we are called to get on stage with our own version of a 104° fever, be it debilitating grief, intense fear, overwhelming uncertainty, or personal health issues. In the midst of those moments, we are still expected to lead ourselves and others toward wellness. During such times, we need to seek help, be transparent with trusted people about what we are struggling with, and be intentional about finding moments for rest, retreat, and reflection as we regain our footing.

When considering a personal pullback in the middle of a crushing season, the temptation is to think, *My company will die if I'm not at 100%*. Be faithful to bring all you have, and trust a good and loving God to be all you are not. We are called to persevere while our God has promised to preserve us.

> Blessed is the one who considers the poor! In the day of trouble the LORD delivers him; the LORD protects him and keeps him alive; he is called blessed in the land; you do not give him up to the will of his enemies. The LORD sustains him on his sickbed; in his illness you restore him to full health. (Psalm 41:1–3)

God will sustain us and our businesses according to His will. Our job is simply to continue being faithful in our calling.

STAYING POWER

Persevering in your calling is not easy. Sometimes it feels like too much to handle. Sometimes you just need to be vulnerable with God's people and ask them for support, as my wife, Shelley, did during a busy and difficult season in our lives.

One night, Shelley came home from a hard women's group meeting. We stayed up late debriefing it together. Through tears, Shelley had unloaded to the group about everything going on in her life. She was overwhelmed. The women comforted her, wrapping their arms around her, loving on her, and sharing some common advice, "You need to take something off your plate."

After Shelley had processed the advice, she shared her conclusion with me before we went to bed: "I actually don't think there is anything I'm supposed to take off my plate."

I told her, "Maybe you're right."

How often do you hear people tell their friends, "I know things are difficult, and I understand what you are going through. You need to persevere. Don't give up. Don't grow weary of doing good. Keep going and be faithful with everything God has given you."

People don't say that.

No, we tell people, "The only option you have is to take something off your plate." As someone who can easily overcommit, I need to hear this advice regularly. A lot of times, it's great advice.

But maybe sometimes life is just hard, and God is calling us to be faithful and persevere. Maybe God is calling you to remain under the pressure and grow there in the furnace.

A pastor once told me that if you take a filthy, dirty rag and just lay it in a raging, flowing river, the river will run it clean. You don't have to wash it. You don't have to rinse it. If you just lay the rag down in the rushing water, it will, over time, simply become clean. That's what happens when we tap into the staying power of perseverance.

Perseverance produces character. It produces faithfulness.

Lay yourself down in the river and just stay there. Persevere in that position, and you'll see the joy-filled fruit of faithfulness flow abundantly from your life and leadership as God runs your life cleaner and cleaner.

FAITHFUL LEADER COMMITMENTS

01 I will persevere by trusting God for the impact of my faithfulness, even when it remains unseen.

02 I will persevere by faithfully confronting challenges rather than avoiding them.

03 I will persevere through discouragement caused by criticism, contempt, or opposition by holding fast to my convictions as a faithful leader.

04 I will persevere by loving and serving others without expecting reciprocation.

05 I will persevere by making difficult decisions guided by integrity and the pursuit of what is right, even in the face of disagreement.

06 I will persevere by finding joy and contentment in my identity in Christ, regardless of external circumstances.

07 I will persevere by embracing the call to endurance, remaining faithful to the end, and trusting God's guidance.

AN ETERNAL CALLING

I know of nothing, dear friends, which I would choose to have, as the subject of my ambition for life, than to be kept faithful to my God to death, still to be a soul-winner, still to be a true herald of the cross, and testify the name of Jesus to the last hour.[60]

CHARLES HADDON SPURGEON

9

GOD IS PLEASED WITH YOU

We are not saved from mediocrity and obscurity, the ordinary and the mundane. We are saved in the midst of it. We are not redeemed from the mundane. We are redeemed from the slavery of thinking our mundane life is not enough.[61]

MATT B. REDMOND

WHEN JARELL AND Shaniya moved to Gainesville for a worship leader position, a mutual friend told us, "You have to meet this family." If you've been married awhile, you understand that finding a couple you and your wife equally enjoy hanging out with can be difficult. Shelley's and my relationship with Jarell and Shaniya became a precious friendship and a breath of fresh air for all of us.

Jarell and I went deep quickly. Over lunch (not tacos, surprisingly), Jarell and I talked about leading worship at our churches, as both of us were worship leaders at the time. We also talked about marriage, previous jobs, kids, pandemic life, and personal struggles. As I shared my story with Jarell, his refrain in response was self-critical and embarrassing for me: "You have accomplished so much . . . and I'm the same age as you!"

We clicked so well that we hung out several times in just the first few weeks of meeting each other. (We even watched *Hamilton* together.)

In one of our Sunday hangout sessions, Jarell shared a voicemail with me that a woman on his worship team had left him after church that day. Among the encouragements that this team member shared, she said, "You have a way of leading worship that's not about performance. I'm excited to be under your leadership." We rejoiced together over how God was moving in his new leadership role.

Later that evening, I took him for a ride in my Tesla and let him drive on the way back. As he drove, Jarell said, "I feel successful. I feel important driving this car. This is what success looks like."

It broke my heart to hear Jarell say that because of how highly I think of him and his gifts. I immediately pushed back and said, "Jarell, this isn't what success looks like. Success looks like that voicemail you received from the woman in your church."

Because our culture praises the people who make a lot of money, own cool things, or accomplish huge feats, we ourselves often think that God deems them "successful," as if they are the people He is most pleased with and upon whom He is pouring out the most blessings.

That's not how God thinks.

> Do not let your adorning be external—the braiding of hair and the putting on of gold jewelry, or the clothing you wear—but let your adorning be the hidden person of the heart with the imperishable beauty of a gentle and quiet spirit, which in God's sight is very precious. For this is how the holy women who hoped in God used to adorn themselves, by submitting to their own husbands. (1 Peter 3:3–5)

Though this verse is written to women, the principle is the same for all of us: lives that honor God are those adorned with hidden things that are inside us, things that create beauty not seen but felt. *Who we are* honors the Lord.

That is not to say that people who accomplish a lot for the Lord do not honor God in doing so. But too often, we convince ourselves that God loves these high achievers more, as though they are God's especially beloved "super saints." We begin to think the measure of God's love and favor depends on how much we do for Him. This is a form of religious outcome-based thinking.

We need to shift our perspective and learn to see ourselves and our accomplishments as God does. He measures us not by our external outcomes but by our faithfulness, our daily hard work entrusted to God.

MOST OF US ARE LYDIA

Our religious outcome-based thinking can get in the way of truly understanding God's heart, even while we're reading His Word. The Bible is full of big stories, grand adventures, and miraculous events: blind people seeing again, people being supernaturally transported from one city to another, donkeys talking, and kings getting swallowed up by worms.

When we read these stories, it can be tempting to think, *Big stories, grand adventures, miraculous events: this is what my life is supposed to look like*. We can start to question why we don't see the same types of things in our lives.

The Bible, however, is largely a collection of the extraordinary. This is an important fact, because it affects how we should read the Bible. When we look at Bible stories and suggest that our lives should look like those people's lives, we are attempting to make the extraordinary the ordinary.

This isn't the point of these stories.

Not everyone is meant to be the apostle Paul.

Not everyone is meant to be the next King Solomon.

Not everyone is meant to be Joshua.

These figures lived extraordinary lives. That's why we're still talking about them thousands of years later.

But for every extraordinary figure in the Bible, there are countless ordinary people—just like us. One example is a businesswoman named Lydia.

After receiving a vision to pursue ministry opportunities in Macedonia, Paul and Timothy first met Lydia while they were hanging out for a few days in Philippi. On the Sabbath, they went down to the river, hoping to find some people to pray with, and there they met Lydia.

If you have read Acts 16 before, you most likely passed over this woman. She probably didn't seem exceedingly worthy of your attention. She sounds pretty vanilla, nothing special.

There are only two verses in the entire Bible that mention her by name. When we meet her, here is what we read:

> One who heard us was a woman named Lydia, from the city of Thyatira, a seller of purple goods, who was a worshiper of God. (Acts 16:14)

Three things stand out to me about Lydia.

First, she was a woman. Women generally lacked prominent positions and voices in the first-century Roman empire. In many ways, New Testament Christianity elevated the status of women in society, recognizing their coequal status before God.

Second, she was an entrepreneur. Lydia's product seems very common to us, but producing purple textiles in AD 32 was extremely difficult. Purple dye was harvested from the glands of sea snails, and dyeing even a small patch of fabric required tens of thousands of snails.[62] Because the dye was difficult to produce, purple garments were expensive and worn only by the wealthy. Lydia would have sold her product to the highest classes in her society. She was gifted at her laborious craft.

Third, people knew her as a worshiper of God. Her reputation as a vendor of fine purple goods would have greatly contributed to her standing, earning her the respect and admiration of the affluent members of society. But, when Luke writes about Lydia, he introduces her as "a worshiper of God."

Lydia worshiped God. She used her gifts to produce innovative products in the market and, eventually, to serve others and fund gospel ministry.

That's a simple life.

That is faithfulness.

Everybody wants to be Elijah and call fire down from heaven.

Everybody wants to be Peter and preach a message that leads to 3,000 people getting saved.

Everybody wants to be David and defeat Goliath.

But most of us won't ever have huge stages, mega influence, or world-changing, window-rattling ministries. But all of us can be faithful with what we have: our gifts and our goods.

Most of us are meant to be Lydia.

That day, when Paul met with Lydia, God opened her heart to pay attention to a message about Jesus. After she was baptized, she turned to Paul and Timothy and begged them:

> If you have judged me to be faithful to the Lord, come to my house and stay. (Acts 16:15)

We need more Lydias in the world: faithful people who invite the work of God into their lives, their families, their homes, and their businesses.

Lydia's story is a simple one about a businesswoman being faithful with everything she has. But her story was so important to God that He made sure it was recorded in history forever.

Our simple, faithful lives dedicated to others and to the Lord are such a great pleasure to God. He doesn't need us to have a huge stage, a giant ministry, a massive company, or a big following. He loves our simple acts of faithfulness.

GOD LOVES THE BELLMAN

When I think of God's pleasure in simple faithfulness, I think of a man I've never met, whom I first heard about in our small group.

Shelley and I have been leading weekly Bible-centered small groups for almost 20 years. The members of our group often bring us ideas about curriculum they think would be helpful to the group. At one point, someone recommended Randy Alcorn's study on heaven, and we decided to use it.

The fourth session was about ruling and reigning in heaven. In the opening video, Alcorn shared about a time he was attending a Christian writer's conference in Atlanta. At his hotel, he met a bellman whom he immediately connected with. The bellman told Alcorn he was praying for him, asking that the Holy Spirit would speak to him during his time at the conference.

To communicate his affection for the man, Alcorn decided to buy him a small gift: a rough wooden cross. When he presented the gift, the bellman was stunned and started to cry. With tears in his eyes, he turned to Alcorn and said, "You didn't have to do that. I'm only a bellman."

Reflecting on the bellman's humble response, Alcorn remarked, "This is the kind of guy who is going to reign in the Kingdom of God: [someone with] a servant's heart. There is nothing 'only' about this guy. There's something special about him. In the Kingdom of God, it would be a privilege for me to carry his bags."[63]

God loves the faithful, quiet leader. He loves ordinary, run-of-the-mill, serving-in-secret, faithful Christians just as much as He does all the "famous," faithful Christians. God loves faithful small- and mid-sized business owners just as much as He does Fortune 500 executives who surrender their lives and leadership to Him.

There are so many bellmen, farmers, social workers, warehouse linemen, janitors, and stay-at-home moms who spend their whole lives serving others and thinking, *I'm only a* . . .

There is no such thing as "only a . . ." in God's economy. That's not a role you can play. You're never "only a teacher" or "only a truck driver" or "only a trainer." Your vocation is simply a vehicle for a much higher calling: faithful ambassador. Put that on your business card.

The psalmist understood this higher calling, writing, "I would rather be a doorkeeper in the house of my God than dwell in the tents of wickedness" (Psalm 84:10). He didn't care where he served God; he'd rather be on the outside of God's temple, just standing at the door, than be unfaithful.

Regardless of your vocational role, your faithfulness pleases your Father.

This is where comparison can be the killer of all joy. If you look at another leader's life, you'll be tempted to think, *But I'm not doing/accomplishing what that leader is.* You are not supposed to! God has equipped every leader uniquely with the skills, opportunities, and influence they have to accomplish His purposes. Faithful leaders content themselves with the portion the Lord has given them. They rejoice in their calling; they don't long for somebody else's.

This is something my friend Jarell has been working through.

One night when Shelley and I hosted Jarell and Shaniya for dinner, Jarell shared openly about how he was feeling the weight of a need to be "successful." He couldn't escape this thought: *What have I accomplished in my life? What am I doing with my life?* I suspect he doesn't realize how common this question is for most people.

In front of his wife, I turned to Jarell and said, "Bro, you have a healthy marriage; you're raising three beautiful black leaders; you get paid to use your musical gifts in the church each weekend to point hundreds to Jesus; and you and your wife get to serve our community in impactful, Christ-centered ways. . . . What else do you want in life? What else do you think is left in life? God is pleased with you."

Like Jarell, you are not called to someone else's level of success and accomplishment. God has a unique plan for you. We don't need to compare ourselves to other leaders, because that is not our method for defining success. Defining success begins with us asking our Shepherd, "What do *You* want to do with my life?"

When we are faithful to pursue whatever small or large plans God has for our lives, we can rest, knowing He is pleased with our faithful obedience.

MY DELIGHT IS IN HER

I often need to be reminded that God is pleased with my faithful obedience. I included one such reminder in a Christmas card I wrote a few years back.

That year, the PHOS team chose to direct their care and attention toward the women who were being served by Created Gainesville, a nonprofit organization seeking to end sex trafficking within our city. The women in their programs have been impacted by sex trafficking and sexual exploitation within our local community and are walking through an intentional process of healing and restoration.

We provided a Scripture-filled journal and handwritten letter to each of the 30 women in Created's program.

I labored over what to write in my note. How do I share something helpful with someone I don't know? I decided to tell her my story for the year.

> This year has been a challenging year for me/everyone in the world. But, in the midst of all the craziness, God has been showing up in my life. He's been teaching me.
>
> It sounds so simple, but the biggest thing He has taught me this year is that He loves me. I knew that, but He taught me again.
>
> He reminded me that He loves me even though I'm so broken. I need reminding because I don't believe it. I find it impossible to understand how and why He would do that.
>
> He feels the same way about you.

You are beautiful in God's eyes. Not because of what you have done or failed to do but because you are His.

You were created for a huge, beautiful, and amazing purpose: to make much of this God who loves you. The crazy thing I learned this year is that He doesn't just love you; He DELIGHTS in you.

I treasure you as a daughter of God, and I rejoice over your worth. All my love.

If you attend a few services at your local Baptist church, you will hear of God's love for you. You might even be given a free, branded bumper sticker with that message on it. Personally, I know God loves me; the message of Jesus suffering on the cross for my sins convinces me of that. But the more the gap between my understanding of God's holiness and my unholiness grows, the more I'm tempted to think that His love is obligatory or demanded, or that it's simply a required emotion to align with His character. Isaiah 62:2–5 paints a different picture:

> The nations shall see your righteousness,
>   and all the kings your glory,
> and you shall be called by a new name
>   that the mouth of the LORD will give.
> You shall be a crown of beauty in the hand of the LORD,
>   and a royal diadem in the hand of your God.
> You shall no more be termed Forsaken,
>   and your land shall no more be termed Desolate,
> but you shall be called My Delight Is in Her,
>   and your land Married;
> for the LORD delights in you,
>   and your land shall be married.
> For as a young man marries a young woman,
>   so shall your sons marry you,
> and as the bridegroom rejoices over the bride,
>   so shall your God rejoice over you.

Spoken to Zion, we see the heart of God for His people in this passage. He doesn't just love His people; He delights in them. You are God's delight! He rejoices over you! If you are a Jesus follower, when you stand before God one day, He won't address you by your birth name. He will instead call you forward with the title on your new name tag:

My Delight Is in Her/Him [Your Name]

That name isn't given to you once you reach a certain level of personal holiness, ministerial success, organizational outcomes, or religious results. Jesus secured that name for you. God delights in you because you are His. It is your adoption that secures the delight of the Father.

His delight isn't reserved for the religious elite, the mega-famous missionaries you've read about, or the world's most generous, mission-minded leaders. God delights in the faithful, regular, broken people who see that there is nothing ordinary about any of the work we do when we are doing that work for the glory of God. All of our work is transmuted from ordinary to heavenly. Our serving becomes a spiritual sacrifice. Our work becomes worship. Our desk becomes an altar of praise. Our lives become vehicles for God's plans. And, as we are faithful, we store up treasures in heaven for ourselves.

There are no "super saint" leaders. We are all called to be faithful in the roles we've been given, and we can be confident that our faithful leadership in every context is a great delight to the Father.

SIT, STAY, LIE DOWN

We want our lives to matter, and we don't want them to be full of mediocrity, so it is natural for us to tell ourselves "I am destined for greatness." Every Disney movie ever created has tried to hype us up to believe that message. I can even hear Uncle Ben telling the future Spider-Man, "If anyone's destined for greatness, it's you, son."

When we adopt this outcome-based mindset, we define success as accomplishing something grandiose and reaching a state of greatness. We need to rewire this aspect of our definition of success.

But the fact is, the roles we're given and the contexts to which God calls us are not always glamorous. Take Ezekiel, for example.

Ezekiel was an Old Testament prophet of God who gave us some of the most significant prophecies in the Bible. In Ezekiel 4, God asked Ezekiel to do some really weird stuff. Among those asks, God tells Ezekiel to lie on his side for over a year with cords wrapped around himself as a sign against Jerusalem. During that time, Ezekiel was to ration his food and bake barley cakes over his own excrement. (God graciously allows him to use cow dung instead.)

Imagine this is your life. Imagine that as you are waiting for clarity from the Lord on your purpose and calling, you finally hear back: "Outside your church, I want you to lie on your side for an entire year, eating some food that you'll bake over cow poop. As people walk by, you'll be a prophetic art installation for them. When you're done, do the same thing again, but lie on your right side for 40 more days."

What did the people think about this prophet of God? What did they think about God?

Were people walking next to this stinking sight shouting, "I'm undone! What must I do to be saved!?" I'm not sure, but I do know that Ezekiel will receive a commendation from the Lord, not because of his results but because of his obedience.

Would you have been obedient if that were God's calling for you?

A friend once challenged me with a similar question: Would you be willing to follow God's plan if He wants you to sit in a chair facing a wall for your whole life? You want to get up, walk around, and explore, but God wants you to simply sit in the chair. You want to build a better chair or dismantle it to get out of the room, but God just wants you to sit in it. Would you be okay with that?

Our hearts are so drawn to greatness and accomplishing the seemingly impossible. God is pleased with our simple obedience. His heart is for us to simply be faithful, even if that means just sitting in the chair, or, as in Ezekiel's case, lying on your side for a year.

JOYFUL INEPTITUDE

God calls us to obey Him—to delight in His calling and faithfully live it out—because He knows we can accomplish nothing on our own.

> I am the vine; you are the branches. Whoever abides in me and I in him, he it is that bears much fruit, for apart from me you can do nothing. (John 15:5)

This verse from John 15 has to be one of the most humiliating lines ever written in the Bible. Apart from God, we can do **nothing**.

We can accomplish nothing . . .
We can control nothing . . .
We can produce nothing . . .
We can gain nothing . . .
We can influence nothing . . .

That is everyone's state apart from God, and it's a pretty bleak picture of learned helplessness. Why in the world would anyone be happy about that verse?

Three words change the whole way we look at this verse: "apart from me."

Many of us question our abilities, and for some, this questioning becomes debilitating. Imposter syndrome is a psychological phenomenon in which the doubt we have about our strengths and the fear we have of our weaknesses becomes so great that we start living out of the fear that one day we'll be outed for our incompetence and labeled an "imposter."

John 15 is calling us to joyfully embrace our ineptitude. A faithful leader should gladly raise his or her hand and say, "Yeah, um, I've actually got nothing of value apart from Jesus." Instead of trying to hide or mask our insufficiencies, we ought to embrace this diagnosis of our helpless condition and rejoice exceedingly more that the Vine has promised to give us all the strength and resources necessary to produce the fruit we so eagerly desire to see.

Andrew Murray says this of the faithful leader:

> His whole heart says Amen to the word: You can do nothing. And just because he does so, he can also say: "I can do all things in Christ who [strengthens] me." The sense of helplessness, and the abiding to which it compels, leads to true fruitfulness and diligence in good works.[64]

In our leadership, let's start by confessing our emptiness, embracing the gifts God has given us, and then faithfully lead others from a place of joyful, confident dependence on Jesus.

BROKENNESS IS THE ONLY QUALIFICATION

If we choose to hide our ineptitude and weakness instead of confessing it and rejoicing that "our" achievements are actually God's, it's probably because we're still defining success by our outcomes. One truly unfortunate consequence of a broken definition of success is the effect it has on peer-to-peer mentorship.

We believe that, in order to be valuable to other people in mentorship, we need to have accomplished a lot in life. We struggle to believe that we are qualified to give advice to someone—because we know all our own mistakes, the poor choices we've made, and our spiritual and professional deficiencies.

As I engaged in a conversation with a faithful female leader at church, we were discussing a bunch of false and harmful teachings she had received from others in the past about parenting children. These teachings had not only negatively influenced her own approach to parenting but also led her to pass on misguided advice to others. With a broken heart, she turned to me and uttered, "I have no idea how I would counsel other parents now."

"What if you just discipled people from right there?" I asked. "What if you just led with all the ways you've failed and the lessons you've learned?"

This leader had so much to offer people from the lessons she'd learned, but she felt that her broken past disqualified her from offering advice to others. The reality is, her broken past was the very thing that God had given her to use to encourage other people.

One of my pastor friends told me that the only leader he would ever hire was someone who "walked with a limp." He only wanted leaders on his team who had been broken, the ones who had felt the sting of betrayal, loss, or disappointment. Why? Because they were humble.

> This is the one to whom I will look: he who is humble and contrite in spirit and trembles at my word. (Isaiah 66:2)

You want to catch God's eye? You want to draw God's attention? Be humble. Do you feel like you're walking with a limp in life because of something traumatic or painful you've been through? Oh, how you are positioned right now for true greatness in the Kingdom of God.

The outcome-based mindset would have us speak lies over ourselves: *My results aren't good enough. I've messed up too many times. I'm a failure. I have nothing to offer others.*

The faithfulness mindset would have us speak this truth over ourselves: *I'm weak, broken, and hurt. That's exactly who God uses. Here am I, Lord, send me.*

We all have something valuable to contribute to the lives of others. God isn't looking for the next world-changing rockstar. He is looking for Lydias, faithful leaders who walk with a limp, who will raise their hand and say, "I don't have much, but all that I have and all that I am are Yours to use, God."

Don't let the outcome-based mindset and an unhealthy definition of success prevent you from investing in others because you don't think you're far enough along to help them. That's a lie. Find someone to invest in, not because of the outcomes you've produced but because you serve a faithful God, who loves to use the bellmen of the world to shine a light on Jesus.

10

HOW THEN SHALL WE LIVE?

Resolved, to be strictly and firmly faithful to my trust, that that, in Prov. 20:6, "A faithful man who can find?" may not be partly fulfilled in me.[65]

JONATHAN EDWARDS

HAYDEN NORRIS HAS been one of the most influential pastors in my life to date. He entered my life at a critical moment when I needed softening around hard edges created by some previous harsh discipleship. Hayden was the guy who taught me what grace and truth looked like lived out together.

During a one-on-one discipleship moment, Hayden and I were discussing unfaithfulness in leadership. He gave me an assignment that his previous pastor had given him. He told me, "If you want to avoid unfaithfulness in your marriage and ministry, grab a card and write out a list of all the things you would lose if you were unfaithful in your marriage. As you write them out, notice how much impact just that one act of unfaithfulness would have on your life."

At home, I spent time thinking through how unfaithfulness would impact my life personally:

- I would lose my marriage.
- I would lose the respect of my children.
- I would lose my position of leading worship.
- I would lose friendships.
- I would lose family relationships.
- I would lose my influence.

What I have seen over the past two decades of walking with Christ and watching faithful and unfaithful leaders is that faithfulness is literally a life-or-death issue.

Unfaithful leadership destroys lives.

It will destroy your marriage. It will wreck your children. It will crumble your business. It will ruin your ministry. It will call into question in the eyes of the public everything that you have said regarding Jesus, the Bible, and the gospel.

Could anything be worth such devastating self-imposed destruction?

IT DOESN'T HAVE TO BE YOU

I remember the first time I was told that someone I respected in ministry had been unfaithful to his wife. I couldn't reconcile the fact that I had received so much good from him. I couldn't make sense of all the great advice and godly counsel he had given me. *What am I supposed to do with all the things I learned from him? Do I just reject everything because he was clearly not walking faithfully with the Lord?*

The second time I saw a faithful leader fall, I thought, *Great, another one! If all the people I learn from and grow under are unfaithful, when will my turn be? Is my own story of unfaithful leadership inevitable?*

Even while writing this book, I received a call from a pastor letting me know that a leader with whom I co-led the worship team for a year announced he was divorcing his wife and had never loved her. My heart was broken.

I'm close friends with the brothers of the woman being divorced, so I FaceTimed them to chat about what was going on and started crying while we discussed the heartache their sister was going through. When the guys asked me how *I* was feeling about the whole situation, I told them about the men I just mentioned above, and, at the end of the FaceTime call, one of them said to me, "Brandon, you need to hear this: this doesn't have to be you."

The world will always be full of unfaithful leaders who will fall off the giant platforms we've erected for them. But just because that's true doesn't mean we will inevitably add our names to that list.

I hope very few people reading this book wreck their lives and those around them with unfaithfulness.

But, the fact is, *all* of us will fail in some way (morally, professionally, relationally, etc.). All of us will be unfaithful. What then?

YET IT WILL ALWAYS BE YOU

I'm not talking about shipwrecking our faith. I'm talking about the regular, unfaithful use of our time, our money, and our platforms. In all the ways that we have discussed being faithful in surrender, perseverance, stewardship, and becoming, we are regularly unfaithful. We choose us, we choose instant gratification, we choose our way, we lose resolve, and we waste our opportunities. We err, we sin, and we fall.

Here is our hope:

> If we are faithless, he remains faithful—for he cannot deny himself.
> (2 Timothy 2:13)

When we are unfaithful, God always remains faithful. He cannot be unfaithful to us, because He cannot be unfaithful to Himself and His character. He cannot deny who He is.

When you are unfaithful, fall again upon your Faithful Friend.

When you are unfaithful, run again to your Faithful Father.

When you are unfaithful, come again to your Faithful Shepherd.

Jesus died for our unfaithfulness. A. W. Tozer reminds us,

> Upon God's faithfulness rests our whole hope of future blessedness. Only as He is faithful will His covenants stand and His promises be honoured. Only as we have complete assurance that He is faithful may we live in peace and look forward with assurance to the life to come. . . . The tempted, the anxious, the fearful, the discouraged may all find new hope and good cheer in the knowledge that our Heavenly Father is faithful. He will ever be true to His pledged word. The hard-pressed sons of the covenant may be sure that He will never remove His loving-kindness from them nor suffer His faithfulness to fail.[66]

God's faithfulness will never fail us, even in our unfaithfulness. Our recurring faithlessness is met with perfect, steadfast, and sure compassion and forgiveness. Fortunately, the level of our faithfulness isn't what commends us to God. He doesn't love us based on whether we've been faithful or not. We won't stand before God at the judgment seat and share stories about how we've been faithful. Heaven will be too full of loud singing over Jesus in celebration of His faithfulness toward us.

MASTER THE RESTART

Given our natural bent toward unfaithfulness, every one of us has to get exceptionally good at pressing the restart button. A pastor in Iowa gave me this phrase: "If you want to live a faithful life, you've got to **master the restart**."

January 1 is a giant global reset button each year. Individuals and businesses take the opportunity to reset their annual goals, projections, and dreams. No matter how horrible the past year has been, when January 1 rolls around, you are happy to say hello to a whole new year ahead. The previous year is only a day behind you, but you feel like something new, different, and better is already here.

Our hope is this: for the Christian, every day is January 1. Every day is a new day. Every day is a chance to restart. We receive new mercies and new grace. You get to wake up every day and commit to a new day of faithful living for Christ.

My church is great about asking this challenging question that gets to the heart of our walk with Jesus:

> How does God feel about you right now?

I counseled a pastor who was helping his wife move into her new apartment after she chose to divorce him, and I asked him this question: "How does God feel about you right now?"

"You want the right answer, or how I *feel* right now?" he asked with one of the first smiles I had seen on his face that day.

I told him the right answer was too easy, so I wanted the real answer.

"If I'm being honest," he paused, "I feel like I'm out in the field . . . but I'm not allowed in the house right now."

These self-imposed feelings of separation are the enemy's tools for preventing us from hitting the reset button. The enemy knows we won't hit the restart button if we feel like we are not allowed to.

I reminded my friend that the Father is standing on the house's porch right now with His arms open wide, calling for him to come back inside. I told him that my concern for his journey ahead was his faithfulness to Christ on the other side of this challenging season.

You are not defined by your past. You can choose to push the restart button.

> Did you fail to love your spouse faithfully yesterday? Love your spouse *today*.
>
> Did you fail to lead your children faithfully yesterday? Lead them well *today*.

Did you fail to respond to a challenging situation at work yesterday in a manner that aligned with your mission, purpose, and values? Apologize and try again *today*.

Nothing is preventing you from waking up tomorrow morning as if it were January 1, except you. Moving forward in faithfulness is going to require you to master the restart.

DO THE NEXT THING

If you're like me, you are both happy and frustrated every time someone misses a meeting with you. On the one hand, you think, *I just got an hour back!* On the other hand, you think, *Dude, I had this time blocked out for you, and I could have met with someone else.*

I had this problem with a pastor from Uganda multiple times. I struggled for a week or two to find a time on my calendar to meet with this pastor to discuss branding for a nonprofit he directs. When we finally got it booked, he missed our virtual call. Strike one.

He apologized profusely, stating that his Wi-Fi was acting up. We rescheduled, and he missed our second call. At that point, I wasn't going to pursue this project any longer.

Three days after our call was scheduled, I received a message from him. His young daughter had been kidnapped and repeatedly raped. She had just been found and was now in the hospital.

There are literally no words.

My petty annoyance immediately melted into a deep heartsickness. I had to let that reality sit with me for a few days before I could even respond to him.

When horror strikes you, your family, or someone you know, what does faithfulness look like? What does it mean to trust God in the bleakest, darkest, and most horrific of seasons?

Elisabeth Elliot knew what it was like to trust God in times of darkness. Her husband, Jim Elliot, was a missionary who was murdered at the hands of the people he was trying to share the gospel with. After his murder, Elisabeth was surrounded by new roles and responsibilities that she would have to take on alone, including caring for her 10-month-old baby.

As Elisabeth leaned into each of the challenges she faced, she would often repeat to herself the words of this old Saxon legend:

> Many a questioning, many a fear,
> Many a doubt, hath its quieting here.
> Moment by moment, let down from Heaven,
> Time, opportunity, and guidance are given.
> Fear not tomorrows, child of the King,
> Trust them with Jesus, *do the next thing*.
>
> Do it immediately, do it with prayer;
> Do it reliantly, casting all care;
> Do it with reverence, tracing His hand
> Who placed it before thee with earnest command.
> Stayed on Omnipotence, safe 'neath His wing,
> Leave all results, *do the next thing*.
>
> Looking for Jesus, ever serener,
> Working or suffering, be thy demeanor;
> In His dear presence, the rest of His calm,
> The light of His countenance be thy psalm,
> Strong in His faithfulness, praise and sing.
> Then, as He beckons thee, *do the next thing*.[67]

Sometimes faithfulness just looks like doing the next thing.

Sometimes the lights seem to go out in life, and it feels like we are walking around blind just trying to hold on to something. Hear the words of this poem: God is "strong in His faithfulness." "Leave all results" and "just do the next thing."

These words are especially crucial when our lives are invaded by grief and pain.

As I sat at the foot of my mom's hospital bed after her passing, I didn't know what to do, so I just journaled while we waited for hospice to arrive. I was struggling with this question, "When do you choose to get up and walk away? What do you walk away to go and do? Dishes? Get a smoothie?"

Sometimes the only thing you can do is hold fast to the God who is carrying you, stand up, and faithfully go and do the next thing.

CONFIDENCE IN MYSTERY

As I was walking through grief after losing my mom, I decided to reach out for professional counseling support.

For years I have told people, "Counseling is a sign of maturity, not weakness," but signing up for my first session, walking in, sitting down, and being vulnerable with my counselor was my first time testing what I preached to be true. *Would I be encouraged or embarrassed if I saw someone I knew there?*

The sessions were extremely valuable, helping to uncover patterns in me that I had not previously seen. During one session, I was unpacking a long journey I had been on to get clarity from the Lord on some decisions I needed to make in life. The counselor asked me how I thought the Lord wanted me to feel on this journey. I said, "Free."

"Brandon, abiding in the Lord feels less certain," she shared. "As much as I hope that you find clarity, my greater hope is that you learn to be more confident in mystery."

As we age, our businesses age, our children age, and our marriages age, the more complex our problems become. I think I knew this, but I didn't consider the effect of this truth on me as a leader. The more complex your problems become, the less clarity you'll have in the solutions you invent. Is this the right thing? Is this the *best* thing? Your certainty in answering those questions can plummet as your problems mature.

God wants us to stay faithful in the mystery. Will we continue to seek Him and abide with Him, even if we are walking through a lot of unknowns, without the full picture, and with less confidence than we've had before? Because you know God, you don't need to fear placing your unknown future in His hands. God knows your future. You can be faithful to keep going, even if you don't have all the answers, because you know the One who does.

ENDGAME SEQUENCE

God wants us to trust Him with the unknowns, but He has told us many things we *can* know. One of those is life's endgame sequence.

Shelley and I love playing board games, especially with other people. Many of our friends are also boardgamers, so we have played a lot of different types of games. A game's end sequence answers the question, "How do we know when the game ends, and what happens once it ends?"

In some games, play continues after the endgame trigger occurs, and all players get one last round of playing, trading resources, or buying goods.

In other games, when the endgame trigger occurs, the game ends immediately, and no more play occurs. That's the endgame sequence for our lives.

When our lives are over and we die, that's it. There are no more final plays, no second chances, no more exchanges, and no make-up exams. It's game over. Hebrews 9:27 says that "it is appointed for man to die once, and after that comes judgment."

You get one life to live.

In his poem "Only One Life," C. T. Studd writes,

> Only one life, 'twill soon be past,
> Only what's done for Christ will last.

At the end of your life, what will be important? Only what's done for Christ. The moment we stand before the throne of God, the Master will have only one of two things to share. He will either tell us,

> I never knew you; depart from me, you workers of lawlessness.
> (Matthew 7:23)
>
> *or*
>
> Well done, good and *faithful* servant. You have been *faithful* over a little; I will set you over much. Enter into the joy of your master.
> (Matthew 25:23, emphasis mine)

We're not waiting to be told, "Well done, good and **fruitful** servant." No, we are aiming to be told, "Well done, good and **faithful** servant." The one great, ultimate question asked over your life will be simple: were you *faithful*?

Did you faithfully come after Me, surrendered to My plan?

Did you faithfully lean into becoming more and more like My Son?

Did you faithfully steward everything I gave you?

Did you faithfully persevere until the end?

Faithfulness. That is what the Master desires of His followers. We are living our whole lives to hear six words: "Well done, good and faithful servant." And, at the heart of that commendation, is Jesus' heart for you to live and lead faithfully in every context of your life.

The call to be faithful is a calling that starts now.

IMPACT YOU CAN'T SEE

I learned a lot about the calling to be faithful with our finances on the longest Zoom call of my life to date (seven and a half hours!). This marathon session was for an online program called a Journey of Generosity (JOG), facilitated by an organization known as Generous Giving. To say the call was life-changing is an understatement.

We spent those seven hours watching stories of people who have shown radical generosity and discussing what the Bible uniquely says about our calling to generosity.

The morning after the JOG, as I was reading my Bible and praying, I felt the need to call Rafael Diaz, a friend of mine who owned a local car dealership.

Rafael picked up the phone. "Mr. West! PHOS Creative, PHOS Creative," he started singing. After we caught up, he asked me why I was calling.

I told him I wasn't entirely sure.

I gave him three reasons why I thought God may have wanted me to call him, but when I shared the third one with him, his answer was simply, "Whoa," then silence.

I told him I thought I might be on the phone with him because someone he had spoken to recently needed help, and God might be connecting us so we can serve that person. Shocked, he told me that, within the past week, a woman he had known for a while called him to share about a difficulty she had been through recently because of the pandemic, and she was without a car to get her to and from work.

After we hung up, I shared the story with Shelley, and she said, "We have to get involved."

I texted Rafael and shared with him, "God is calling us to serve this woman. We would like to purchase a car for her. Can you show me some options that you would personally consider for your own family?"

Rafael delivered the gift anonymously, but we requested that a letter we wrote be delivered with the car, explaining why we did this and sharing God's love with her.

The day following Rafael's delivery of the car and letter, he forwarded me a message from her expressing her gratitude. I had more joy that day in my heart than I had experienced in months. God was at work. I thought that was where the story would end, and I was grateful to have been a part of it.

A week later, Rafael forwarded me an email from the new car owner:

> Let him know that I've shared his letter with my WHOLE family. A move of GOD for them to see his greatness and to transform them. I pray they meet Jesus. I've also shared it with my neighbor and some close friends. While I've been reading it, I've been praying that it hits hearts. AND IT HAS. My neighbor who just battled cancer and has fallen on her faith nearly cried and got goosebumps. I saw it. . . . I will never get rid of that car. It will serve as a lifetime testimony that really changed my life. Thank you.

A friend informed me that she still keeps a laminated copy of our letter in her glove compartment to this day. Whenever she is doubting God, she pulls out the letter to remind herself of God's goodness.

Who knows what God will do through your faithfulness? You may never get to know. Maybe your act of faithfulness is not even intended for the person to whom you are demonstrating faithfulness.

An ancient proverb reminds us, "Blessed are those who plant trees under whose shade they will never sit." Faithful leaders persevere in their calling, unsure of the results and impact their work will produce.

ALWAYS WATCHING

When I worked for the University of Florida in the academic technology department, I was able to share Jesus with a man I worked with. He was frustrated with me sharing the gospel but asked how long I had been a Christian. I told him it had been four years since I started my relationship with Jesus.

As we walked around the campus together, he said to me, "You've only been a Christian for a short period of time. Come and see me after you've done this Jesus thing for 15 years, then we'll talk again, and I'll believe you."

What I found so interesting about his comment was the way he was defining my success. For him, the validity and trustworthiness of what I had to say was based on my faithfulness to Jesus. Would I stay true? Would this thing that excited me so much back then excite me a decade later? After I had been through everything he had been through in life, would I still treasure Jesus?

Acts 16 says that right after Paul and Silas met Lydia, they cast a demon out of a fortune-teller slave girl. Her owner became livid and incited the leaders of the city to beat them harshly, throw them in prison, and bind their feet.

At midnight, instead of complaining about their situation, Paul and Silas were singing and praying to God. As they did so, "the prisoners were listening to them" (Acts 16:25). The prisoners could have been yelling at them and demanding they be quiet, but, instead, they were sitting there listening.

Sooner or later, staying faithful, especially when no one sees why you should, just may draw someone to Jesus.

My church currently rents our Sunday meeting space from the Center for Jewish Student Life, or the Hillel, at the University of Florida. When we were looking for space options, the opportunity arose, and we called the rabbi at the Hillel, curious how he would respond. As we pitched the offer to him, he asked again what church we were from.

"Salt Church, sir," we responded.

"Do you have someone who goes to your church named Lucas?" the Rabbi responded.

"We do."

"Lucas is the kindest person I have ever met," he shared. "If there are more people like him in this church, I'll give you anything you want."

During our second weekend in the Hillel, I took Lucas out on the balcony that looks out over the University of Florida (the people we are trying to reach at Salt), and I encouraged Lucas on how God used his faithfulness to advance ministry here at UF.

Who are the people right around you watching, wondering, and listening to see how you'll respond to the best and worst parts of life?

In your house, in your business, in your community group, on your volunteer board, or at the grocery store, there's always somebody observing you, waiting to see if you'll be faithful to the beliefs you espouse. And they're not just watching you to see what you think; they're watching you to see how you *act*. This is especially true of your kids.

> Sometimes our children will fail to listen to us. Rarely will they fail to imitate us.[68]

Be faithful in every season. Your faithful conduct (or your unfaithfulness met with genuine repentance) may be a tool the Lord uses in the lives of those around you.

A STEADY, DAILY STRIDE

Living faithfully is not easy. I'm envisioning a *Lord of the Rings* meme now with Boromir saying, "One does not simply walk into faithfulness." It is too high a calling to assume that you will look back years and decades from now and, without any effort, be able to say, "Yeah, I think I've lived a faithful life."

It's a long-term commitment for which discipline is required.

Faithfulness is listed as a fruit of the Spirit and, as such, is reaped from a harvest of faithful living with Jesus (Galatians 5:22–23). A faithful life is going to require a faithful walk, a steady stride in the same direction.

I blow it so often. I can do the hard work to untie my identity from my outcomes and I go live out of a faithfulness-centered mindset, but then I go and retie myself to the same anchor I just saw myself freed from.

This rinse-and-repeat cycle, though frustrating, is part of our long obedience in the same direction, our faithful following of Jesus in and out of seasons and in and through hardship.

John Rinehart, founder of Gospel Patrons, wrote this prayer in his book *Giving Together*. What a beautiful vision of surrender for the faithful leader:

> Father in Heaven, I choose to believe you today that my identity is not found in being a successful person or a failure, in being wealthy or needy. At my core, I am more than the roles I play, more than a father or a mother, a husband or a wife, a son or a daughter. God, I release to you my desire to base my identity in my performance or what other people say about me. In you, God, I am more than my career or calling, more than my abilities or accomplishments. I release to you all the ways I strive to find identity apart from you, Father. Please, bring me back to the truth of who you are and who I am.[69]

Success isn't defined by something outside you. It is defined by something inside you, and it is assessed by Someone who walks alongside you. Jesus hasn't left you alone as you walk down this long road. He is worth your faithfulness and will never leave you as you cling to Him.

THE CROWN OF LIFE

For people living out of an outcome-based mindset, life is about production. Their definition of success usually looks something like this:

I'll be successful ***when*** I _____.

They might not say this, but this is how they live. When these fill-in-the-blank answers aren't reached, there's frustration, and, when the answers *are* reached, fulfillment is fleeting, as the person chases the next "when I . . ." outcome.

A friend of mine was once hanging out with a visual effects artist from Hollywood, reviewing some of the awards on his shelf. This artist had worked on some of the largest movies to ever hit the big screen, had received several Academy Award nominations, and had just won his first Oscar. He described the joy of winning his Oscar, celebrating with world-renowned producers at the after-party, and coming home that night to put the award on his shelf.

"What'd you do the next day?" my friend asked.

With a melancholy look, the artist described how empty that next day felt. "I went back to work," he shared. "And I told myself, 'I guess I'll try and get my next one.'"

The outcome-based mindset is a forever-moving finish line and an endless cycle of downhill living and disappointments. Even if you get the results you want, then what?

The faithfulness mindset is flipping this paradigm. It's a subtle change with colossal consequences, and it looks like this:

I'll be successful *as* I _____.

Faithfulness defines success not as a place reached or as a goal accomplished but *as a heart posture sought and a consistent lifestyle lived.*

All of your life belongs on the line above.

I'll be successful *as* I faithfully love people who are hard to love.

I'll be successful *as* I faithfully live for God in the midst of painful seasons.

I'll be successful *as* I faithfully steward my resources for others.

I'll be successful *as* I faithfully surrender to God's plans in my becoming.

What if we willingly resigned ourselves to our results, and daily surrendered our hard work to God?

What if success was not about what you did but *how* you did it and *why* you did it?

It is not your business to succeed, but only to do good, to live faithfully, to do the hard work, and to trust God. That truth gives you the freedom to rest, the courage to take risks, and the strength to keep going when darkness seems to hide His face. You're being carried; you're simply called to live faithfully for the One holding you.

> Be faithful unto death, and I will give you the crown of life. (Revelation 2:10)

NOTES

[1] Mark Cole, "Leading People to Accept Change," John C. Maxwell [blog], November 1, 2019, https://www.johnmaxwell.com/blog/mark-cole-leading-people-to-accept-change/.

[2] C. S. Lewis to Arthur Greeves, letter, in *Yours, Jack: Spiritual Direction from C. S. Lewis* (New York: HarperCollins, 2018), 45.

[3] Andrew Murray, "The Branch," in *The True Vine: Meditations for a Month on John 15:1–16* (Chicago: Moody Press, 1898), https://ccel.org/ccel/murray/true_vine/true_vine.i.html.

[4] "God Moves in a Mysterious Way," William Cowper, 1774.

[5] William Carey, quoted in Mary E. Farwell, *The Life of William Carey* (Woman's Presbyterian Board of Missions of the Northwest, 1888), 17.

[6] *Most*, directed by Bobby Garabedian (Eastwind Films, 2003).

[7] Job 37:16; Psalm 139:4; 147:5; 1 John 3:20.

[8] Corrie ten Boom, *Tramp for the Lord* (Fort Washington, PA: CLC Publications, 1974), 116.

[9] Edward Mote, "My Hope Is Built on Nothing Less," (1834).

[10] *Strong's Exhaustive Concordance of the Bible*, s.v. "faithful," https://www.blueletterbible.org/lexicon/g4103/kjv/tr/0-1/.

[11] Dorothy Kelley Patterson, *A Handbook for Ministers' Wives: Sharing the Blessing of Your Marriage, Family, and Home* (Nashville: B&H Books, 2002), 104.

[12] James Clear, *Atomic Habits: An Easy & Proven Way to Build Good Habits & Break Bad Ones* (New York: Penguin Publishing, 2018), 262.

[13] Henry Cloud, *Necessary Endings: The Employees, Businesses, and Relationships That All of Us Have to Give Up in Order to Move Forward* (New York: HarperCollins, 2011), 229–230.

[14] "Waiting Room," track 7 on Shane and Shane, *Psalms*, 2002.

[15] Jerry Bridges, *Trusting God* (Colorado Springs: NavPress, 2016), 137.

[16] Shola Richards, "GLS21 Notes: Require Civility to Lead," Global Leadership Network, accessed September 27, 2023, https://globalleadership.org/articles/leading-others/gls21-notes-require-civility-to-lead/.

[17] Buffalo Culture (website), C12, accessed September 27, 2023, https://buffaloculture.com/.

[18] Garry Ridge, conference session, May 2022, Purpose Summit.

[19] Oswald Chambers, *My Utmost for His Highest*, updated edition (Grand Rapids, MI: Our Daily Bread Publishing, 2010), 143.

20 Dave Harvey, "What's Your Ambition's Agenda?," Articles, Crossway, January 6, 2019, https://www.crossway.org/articles/whats-your-ambitions-agenda/.

21 Vince Vitale, "Conversation As a Spiritual Discipline," C12, YouTube video, 4:06, https://www.youtube.com/watch?v=5xZy_9_RT3A.

22 John Piper, quoted in C. J. Mahaney, "Strong as Death: The Enduring Power of Covenant Love" in *Sex, Romance, and the Glory of God: What Every Christian Husband Needs to Know* (Wheaton, IL: Crossway, 2018), 98–99.

23 Piper, quoted in Mahaney, *Sex, Romance, and the Glory of God*, 98.

24 C12, "The Ministry of a Leader's Marriage: Reflecting the Covenant of God in Our Relationships," Ministry, (August 2019), 14.

25 Dan Walters, personal communication with author.

26 "Lead Me," track 4 on Sanctus Real, *Pieces of a Real Heart*, 2010.

27 Jeremy Riddle, *The Reset: Returning to the Heart of Worship and a Life of Undivided Devotion* (Anaheim, CA: Wholehearted Publishing, 2020).

28 Gary Thomas, *Cherish: The One Word That Changes Everything for Your Marriage* (Grand Rapids, MI: Zondervan, 2017), 25.

29 Thomas, *Cherish*, 43.

30 Thomas Watson, "A Godly Man Is a Humble Man" in *The Godly Man's Picture* (London: Stephen Walbrook, 1758), 71, https://www.google.com/books/edition/The_Godly_Man_s_Picture_Drawn_with_a_Scr/dpc8KvX84fsC?hl=en&gbpv=1.

31 This quote is widely attributed to Corrie ten Boom, but its source is unclear.

32 "A Covenant with God," The Methodist Covenant Prayer, The Methodist Church, accessed September 27, 2023, https://www.methodist.org.uk/about-us/the-methodist-church/what-is-distinctive-about-methodism/a-covenant-with-god/.

33 Kevin DeYoung, *Just Do Something: A Liberating Approach to Finding God's Will* (Chicago: Moody Publishers, 2014), 93.

34 John Spence, "The Leader of the Future," February 2019, TEDxGainesville, https://www.ted.com/talks/john_spence_the_leader_of_the_future.

35 Global Leadership Network, "Craig Groeschel on Whether Leaders Should Unmake Promises," YouTube video, 1:37, October 12, 2021, https://www.youtube.com/watch?v=Ku6c58Rgk88.

36 *While I'm Waiting*, Reunion Records, 2009. Quoted with John Waller's permission.

37 Dave Harvey, *Rescuing Ambition* (Wheaton, IL: Crossway, 2010), 73–74.

38 Corrie ten Boom, *The Hiding Place* (Royal Oak, MI: Chosen Books, 2006), 44.

39 Nassim Nicholas Taleb, *Antifragile: Things That Gain from Disorder*, Incerto 3 (New York: Random House Publishing, 2014), 3.

40 Encyclopaedia Britannica Online, s.v. "Hydra," accessed August 16, 2023, https://www.britannica.com/topic/Hydra-Greek-mythology.

41 *Journey of Generosity* [online booklet], v. 23.1, Generous Giving, n.d., generousgiving.org

42 Dane Ortlund, *Gentle and Lowly: The Heart of Christ for Sinners and Sufferers* (Wheaton, IL: Crossway, 2020), 138.

43 Martin Luther, "Defense and Explanation of All the Articles," in *Luther's Works, Volume 32: Career of the Reformer II*, eds. George W. Forell & Helmut T. Lehman (Minneapolis, MN: Fortress, 1958), 24.

44 Quoted in Randy Alcorn, "Investing In Eternity," Eternal Perspectives Ministries, March 29, 2010, https://www.epm.org/resources/2010/Mar/29/investing-eternity.

45 CFI Team, "Friedman Doctrine," Corporate Finance Institute, last modified December 5, 2022, https://corporatefinanceinstitute.com/resources/equities/friedman-doctrine/.

46 Mike Sharrow, "Kingdom Torque," CURRENT'21, May 7, 2021, Hyatt Regency Grand Cypress, Orlando, Florida. Watch Sharrow's talk online at https://www.joinc12.com/videos/kingdom-torque/.

47 David Platt, *Radical: Taking Back Your Faith from the American Dream* (Colorado Springs: Multnomah Books, 2010), 216–217.

48 Mary E. Farwell, *The Life of William Carey* (Chicago: Women's Presbyterian Board of Missions of the Northwest, 1888), 17.

49 Saint Patrick, The Confession of Saint Patrick, quoted at "Quotable Quote," Patrick of Ireland, GoodReads, https://www.goodreads.com/quotes/754666-i-pray-to-god-to-give-me-perseverance-and-to.

50 Austin Channing Brown, *I'm Still Here: Black Dignity in a World Made for Whiteness* (Colorado Springs: Convergent Books, 2018), 181.

51 John MacArthur, *Welcome to the Family: What to Expect Now That You're a Christian* (Nashville: Thomas Nelson, 2008), 85–86.

52 This quote is commonly attributed to C. S. Lewis or Neal A. Maxwell, but I could not find a definitive source.

53 Timothy Keller, *Forgive: Why Should I and How Can I?* (New York: Viking Press, 2022), 68.

54 The information in this section about Allen Gardiner and his missions is adapted from John W. Marsh and W. H. Stirling, *The Story of Commander Allen Gardiner, R.N.* (London: James Nisbet & Co., 1883), online via Project Canterbury, http://anglicanhistory.org/sa/gardiner/marsh/.

55 "Allen Gardiner," ed. JAD, GFA Missions, June 4, 1997, https://gfamissions.org/allen-gardiner/.

56 John W. Marsh and W. H. Stirling, *The Story of Commander Allen Gardiner*.

57 *Unraveling*, Bethel Music, 2020, https://bethelmusic.com/resources/to-love-a-fool/unraveling.

58 Sadie Robertson Huff, "GLS20 Session Notes: Forces That Affect Your Influence," Global Leadership Network, accessed September 27, 2023, https://globalleadership.org/articles/leading-others/session-notes-forces-that-affect-your-influence/.

59 C. S. Lewis, *A Grief Observed* (San Francisco: HarperOne, 2015).

60 Charles Haddon Spurgeon, "Enduring to the End," sermon, February 14, 1864, online at The Spurgeon Center, https://www.spurgeon.org/resource-library/sermons/enduring-to-the-end-2/.

61 Matthew B. Redmond, *The God of the Mundane: Reflections on Ordinary Life for Ordinary People* (Minneapolis, MN: Cruciform Press, 2021).

62 Kelly Grovier, "Tyrian Purple: The Disgusting Origins of the Colour Purple," Art History, BBC, August 1, 2018, https://www.bbc.com/culture/article/20180801-tyrian-purple-the-regal-colour-taken-from-mollusc-mucus.

63 Randy Alcorn, "Heaven: The Official Study Guide Video Series," DVD. Available at https://store.epm.org/heaven-the-official-study-guide-dvd/.

64 Andrew Murray, "You Can Do Nothing," in *The True Vine: Meditations for a Month on John 15:1–16* (Chicago: Moody Press, 1898), https://ccel.org/ccel/murray/true_vine/true_vine.i.html.

65 Jonathan Edwards, "The Resolutions of Jonathan Edwards," August 17, 1723, online at Desiring God, https://www.desiringgod.org/articles/the-resolutions-of-jonathan-edwards.

66 A. W. Tozer, *The Knowledge of the Holy* (New York: HarperOne, 2009), 81.

67 Elisabeth Elliot, quoted in Justin Taylor, "Do the Next Thing," Blogs, The Gospel Coalition, October 25, 2017, https://www.thegospelcoalition.org/blogs/justin-taylor/do-the-next-thing/.

68 Randy Alcorn, *Managing God's Money: A Biblical Guide* (Carol Stream, IL: Tyndale House Publishers, 2011), 219.

69 John Rinehart, *Giving Together: An Adventure in Generosity* (n.p.: Reclaimed Publishing, 2023), 35.

www.ingramcontent.com/pod-product-compliance
Lightning Source LLC
Chambersburg PA
CBHW070537090426
42735CB00013B/3008